Alexander Herzen

My Exile in Siberia

Volume 1

Herzen, Alexander

My Exile in Siberia
Volume 1

ISBN: 978-3-86267-019-2
First published in 2010 by Europaeischer Literaturverlag, Bremen, Germany.

Europaeischer Literaturverlag (www.elv-verlag.de), Fahrenheitstr. 1, D-28359 Bremen.

My Exile in Siberia

Volume 1

PREFACE

In order to write down one's own recollections, it is by no means necessary either to be a great man, or an extraordinary villain; a celebrated artist, or a statesman; it is enough to be merely a man, to have something to tell, and to be able and willing to tell it.

Every existence is interesting; if not on account of the person, yet on account of the country, the epoch in which he lives. Man likes to penetrate into the inward life of another; he likes to touch the most delicate chord of another heart, to watch its beatings, and penetrate its secrets, in order to compare, to verify, to seek a justification, a consolation, a proof of conformity.

Memoirs, however, can be tiresome, the life of which they speak can be poor, insignificant. Then do not read them; that is the heaviest punishment to be inflicted upon a book. And as to that, no special right for writing Memoirs can avail. The Memoirs of Benvenuto Cellini are not so interesting on account of his having been a great artist, but because the things he had to relate were most interesting.

"The right to this or that kind of words", is an expression which no longer belongs to our time, but to the time of a minority of intelligence, of the poets-laureate, of the doctors in caps, of the philosophers by privilege, of the patented learned men, and other pharisees of the academical world. In those times, the art of writing was considered sacred, the "official author", not only with the pen, but always speaking in a florid style, chose the most unnatural turning of phrases, and employed the words least used, in a word, he preached, or he sang.

For us, we speak quite plainly. We imagine that writing is an occupation fit for a layman, for any one else, a work like every other work. Here, at least, "the right of labour" cannot be doubted. If the production will find consumers — is another question.

A year ago, I published in London, a part of my Memoirs, in the Russian language, under the title, "Prison and Exile". This work appeared, when war had already begun, and when the means of communication with Russia had become much more difficult. It did not, therefore, expect great success. But it happened otherwise. In the month of September, the "Revue des Deux Mondes", gave long extracts from my book, with a very flattering article about myself, (although I do not share the author's opinions.) In the months of January, other fragments, (likewise translated from the Russian,) appeared in the "Athenaeum" of London, while Hoffman and Campe published a German translation of the work at Hamburg. This has decided me to publish another volume.

I shall say in another place what deep interest these Memoirs have for me individually, and for what purpose I have begun to write them. I now content myself with the assertion: that there is no country in which Memoirs can be more useful than in Russia. We — thanks to the censorship — are very little accustomed to publicity; it frightens, astonishes and offends us. It is time the Imperial artists of the police of St. Petersburg, should know, that sooner or later, their actions, so well hidden by the prisons, the irons and the graves, will be revealed in the broad glare of day.

INTRODUCTION

The Author of the following Memoirs has occupied, since the year 1839, one of the most distinguished places in the literature of his country. Since 1848, his name has also become known in the Literatures of France and Germany. Madame Pulszky, in the Preface to a Russian Novel, entitled "The Hero of our Days", which she has translated into English, speaks of Herzen as "a distinguished Russian refugee, who endeavours to blend German philosophy, French political theory, and English practical common sense, with his original Russian nature."

While Herzen was in Russia, writing under the surveillance of the Tsar, he published his works under the pseudonym "Iskander" (the Turkish form of his Christian name, Alexander); for the Tsar did not allow persons condemned on political grounds (among the number of whom Herzen had found himself from his twenty-first year, as will be seen from the present volumes) to come forward in literature, either under their real names, or with their real rank in society.[1]

All the works which Herzen published in Russia had the tendency of arousing the Russian public from their apathy in regard to their general interests. An apathy which is the chief cause of their supporting a despotic government, and still maintaining the institution of serfdom. As he did not dare to speak openly on political subjects, Herzen published his views under various disguises: sometimes in professed Treatises on Philosophy, such as "Dilettantism in Science", "Letters on the Study of Nature", "On the Historical Development of the Notion of Honour", &c.; at other times as Tales and Novels, such as "Whose Fault is it?", "Memoirs of a Physician", "The Thievish Magpie", "The Journal of a Young Man", &c. No Russian writer before Herzen had treated questions of philosophy with that

---

[1] Thus Bestoujeff, the renowned conspirator of 1825, was obliged to publish his novels under the pseudonym Marlinsky. When an edition of his works was published, accompanied by a portrait of the author, dressed in the uniform of a common soldier, to which low rank he had been degraded, the Chief of the Secret Police was dismissed from his place for allowing this edition to appear.

lively facility which denotes that the author is perfectly familiar with his subject.

> *"Everything that is perfectly understood, will be easily explained.*
> *And the words for expressing it come with facility."*
>
> Boileau

It must not be supposed, however, that either the philosophical or belletristic writings of Herzen, presented the Russian public with an easy and entertaining species of reading. On the contrary, each of his sentences affords matter for reflection; the reader feels at every line, that only half of the author's idea is expressed, and that the other half is left for him to guess. Herzen's talents being perfectly suited to the serious and difficult task which he had proposed to himself, the affection with which he was regarded by his countrymen, was not at all like the attachment generally felt towards distinguished literary men; his works were esteemed in Russia, even more as national services, than as aesthetical productions.

After having been annoyed and persecuted by the Tsar, almost without intermission, from 1834 till 1846,[2] Herzen at last succeeded, in the year 1847, in obtaining a passport to other European countries; and he was thus enabled to be an eye-witness of the revolutionary drama enacted in France and Italy, in 1848. The impressions this spectacle left on his mind, were reproduced in a book entitled "Letters from France and Italy". The reflections this revolution suggested to him, are contained in another work, entitled "From the other Shore", also published in Germany, and which created a great sensation in that country. It was not from any desire to make a name for himself in the literature of Western Europe, that Herzen thus launched him-

---

[2] For instance, Herzen's mother had a considerable sum of money deposited in the Bank of Moscow. After Herzen's departure, Nicholas forbad the authorities of the bank to deliver it to her, and it was only after a protracted correspondence that the firm of Rothschild succeeded, by menaces, in recovering it. Out of revenge, the government of Nicholas seized a sum of ten thousand francs which had been dispatched to Herzen from Russia by his brother. And all this was done to induce Herzen to return to Russia, after 1848.

self as a writer in the German and French languages; but because the Tsar had, since February, 1848, prohibited the publication, in Russia, of anything from his pen. The German press, becoming more and more restricted, Herzen then published, in French, his two works, "On the Development of Revolutionary Ideas in Russia", and "The Russian People and Socialism".[3]

But scarcely had the first of these remarkable works begun to circulate in Paris ere the sale of Herzen's works was prohibited in that capital, as it had previously been at Petersburg; and it is only since the opening of the present war, that the abovementioned books are again to be seen exposed in the window of the bookseller, M. Frank.

Having thus had the gag put upon his mouth everywhere, in Russia, Germany, and France, and persevering in his desire to unveil the ignominy of the Tsar, and to arouse the Russian people from their torpor, Herzen has come to settle in England; and has established in London, at 36, Regent's-square, *the first Free Russian printing-press*. Two years have not yet elapsed since the establishment of this press, and already many thousand copies of Herzen's works have been introduced into Russia by smuggling, and by the generous assistance of the Polish democrats. In addition to some pamphlets amongst which the most striking is "A Summons to the Russian Soldiers in Poland", which was reprinted in the "Daily News" of the 21st April, 1854, and a small brochure, on the subject of serfdom in Russia, entitled "The Baptized Property". Herzen has found time to publish at London in the Russian language three volumes: "Interrupted

---

[3] This work is spoken of in terms of high commendation, by the celebrated French historian, Michelet, in his "Democratic Legends of the North". He there says of Herzen: "The author writes oar language with an heroic vigour, which breaks through his anonymous disguise, and everywhere reveals the true patriot. I have read it, and re-read it, over and over again, with a feeling amounting almost to stupefaction. Methought I saw one of the ancient heroes of the north tracing with a merciless rod of iron the sentence of this miserable world... Alas! it is not the condemnation of Russia only; it is that of France and of Europe also. 'We flee from Russia', he says, 'but Russia is everywhere — Europe is one great prison.' So long, however, as Europe possesses such men as the author, everything may be hoped." — Democratic Legends of the North, p. 125.

Tales", noticed in the "Revue des Deux Mondes" of the 15th July, 1854 the volume here translated, of which also the Revue des Deux Mondes" gave an analysis in its number for the 15th September, 1854; and a Russian edition of the "Letters from France and Italy", already mentioned.

We regret that Herzen did not earlier seek the hospitable soil of England, in order that he might there erect his battery against the galling despotism of Russia, and thus promote the general interests of humanity.

CONTENTS OF THE FIRST VOLUME

CHAPTER I.

The Prophecy — N.'s Imprisonment — The Conflagration — The Muscovite Liberal — M. E. Orloff — The Churchyard

CHAPTER II.

The Arrest — The Police Office — The Patriarchal Tribunal

CHAPTER III.

The Watchtower — The Lisbon Commissioner — The Incendiaries

CHAPTER IV.

The Krutin Barracks — Tales of the Gendarmes — The Officers

CHAPTER V.

The examination — Galitzin, Senior — Galitzin, Junior — General Staal — The Sentence — Sokolofsky

CHAPTER VI.

Exile — The Police-Master at Pokrov — The Wolga — Perm.

CHAPTER VII.

Wiatka — The Office and Dining-Room of His Excellency K. S. Tufeyeff

CHAPTER VIII.

The Civil Officials — The Governor-Generals in Siberia — A Rapacious chief of Police — A Tame Judge — A Roasted Commissioner — A Tatar Apostle — A Boy of the Feminine Gender — The Potato Revolution.

CHAPTER IX.

Alexander Witberg

CHAPTER I

The Prophecy — N.'s Imprisonment — The Conflagration — The Muscovite Liberal — M. P. Orloff — The Churchyard

In the spring of the year 1834, I called one morning at Vadim's. Neither he, his brothers, nor his sisters were at home. I went up stairs into a little room, and sat down to write.

Presently, the door opened softly, and an old woman entered: it was Vadim's mother. Feeble and decrepid, she approached my arm-chair with scarcely audible steps, and said: "Write on — don't disturb yourself; I only came to see if Vade had returned. The children are gone out for a walk. It is so lonely down stairs, that it quite frightened me. I will sit down here for a little while, but I will not disturb you. Go on with your work."

Her face was thoughtful, expressing even more than usual the sufferings of the past, the forebodings of the future, and that distrust in the events of life - which is always the result of great and numerous vexations and misfortunes. We began to talk. She told me many things concerning Siberia.

"Many sorrows have fallen to my lot", she added, shaking her head; "what shall I yet experience — not much that is good, I have a foreboding."

I then remembered how often the old lady had listened to our bold democratic conversations; how she had turned pale, and with a sigh had stolen away from the room, and remained silent for a long time afterwards.

"You and your friends", she continued, "are going straight to perdition. You will plunge Vade, yourself, and all the others into the abyss. I love you no less than my own son."

And tears rolled down her careworn cheeks. I remained silent. She took my hand and said, as she endeavoured to smile:

"Don't be angry; my nerves are weakened, but I understand it all. Go your own way: for you there is no other, and if there were, none of your friends would be what you are. I know it all; but I cannot overcome my anxiety. I have experienced so many misfortunes, that my strength is not sufficient to withstand a new one. But say not a word about it to Vade; it would give him pain, and he would try to convince me. There he comes", she added, hastily wiping away her tears, and once more entreating me, by a sign, to be silent.

Good, pious mother! great, holy woman! does not that equal Corneille's famous "*qu'il mourût?*"

Her prophecy was but too soon fulfilled; although the first storm fortunately passed over her house, still much grief and anxiety were in store for her.

"What! they have arrested him?" I exclaimed, springing out of bed, and passing my hand across my eyes, as if to discover whether I were dreaming or not.

"The Commissary of Police came in the night, two hours after you had left us, accompanied by a police-officer and several Cossacks. They arrested our master, and seized all his papers."

It was N.'s valet who told me this.

I could not imagine what pretext the police could have had. For some time past, everything had been perfectly quiet. N. had only arrived that evening; and why arrest him, and not me? I could not stand by with folded arms. I hastily put on my clothes, and quitted the house without any fixed plan. This was the first misfortune that had befallen me. I loved N. passionately, as men seldom love even in youth. My heart was heavy; the sense of my inability to help him tormented me.

Whilst thus lingering about the streets, I at last bethought me of an acquaintance, whose position in society gave him the means of ascertaining the real state of affairs, and who possibly might even render me some assistance. He lived at a great distance in the country, beyond the Woronzof fields. I stepped into the first coach I could find, and hastened to his house. It was about seven o'clock' in the morning.

We had been acquainted with W. for about a year-and-a-half. He was one of the lions of Moscow. He had been educated in Paris, possessed high intellectual powers, and a well-stored mind, was a free-thinker, witty, and wealthy; and he had been among the number of those who were imprisoned on the 14th of December, and afterwards set at liberty. He had not suffered the actual fate of an exile, yet he enjoyed the glory of one. He was in the service of the state, and exercised a great influence over the chief Governor. Prince Galitzin liked to receive people of liberal views, particularly when views were expressed in good French, as he was not a very first-rate Russian scholar.

W. was about ten years our senior; he had gained our admiration by his practical views, his knowledge of political, affairs, his distinguished powers as an orator in the French language, and his zealous attachment to liberal principles. His knowledge was so comprehensive and exact; he set it forth in so simple and agreeable a manner; he expressed his opinions with so much energy. He was never at a loss for an answer, and was ever ready with his advice or his decision. He read everything that came from the press — new novels, treatises, journals, poetry; besides which, he occupied himself with the study of zoology, wrote essays for the Prince, and sketched the plans for children's books. His liberalism was that of the tricolor party, in its purest form, with a tinge of the principles known as those of the Extreme Left. He occupied a position between Mauguin and General Lamarque.

On the walls of his study were to be seen the portraits of all the revolutionary celebrities, from Hampden and Bailly to Fieschi and Armand Carrel. A whole library of prohibited books was placed under this revolutionary altar. A skeleton, some stuffed birds, some dried amphibia, and the intestines of various animals preserved in spirits, threw a stern shade of contemplation and thought over the otherwise too revolutionary appearance of the apartment.

We envied him his experience, and his knowledge of men; we felt ourselves under the influence of his refined irony; he appeared to us to be a practical revolutionist, and a statesman in spe.

I found, on my arrival, that W. was away from home — he had already driven to see the Prince; but his valet thought he would be back in an hour and a half, so I waited for him.

W.'s country-house was charming. The cabinet in which I waited was a spacious and lofty apartment, situated on the ground-floor, with a wide door opening on a terrace, which led to the garden. It was a sultry day; perfumes were wafted in from the flowers and foliage in the garden; his children were playing and laughing heartily in front of the house. Here were wealth, plenty, space, sunshine, shade, verdure, and flowers; in the prison there are none of these — it is narrow, dim, and suffocating.

I do not know how long I sat plunged in gloomy contemplation; but, all at once, the valet, much excited, called me out on the terrace.

"What is the matter?" I asked.

"Do but come, if you please, and see."

I would not offend him; so went out, and was struck with astonishment. A whole row of houses was in flames, as if all had been kindled at once. The fire spread with incredible rapidity.

I remained standing on the terrace; this aspect of destruction and of unbounded fury was welcome to me. The *valet-de-chambre* looked at the conflagration with a kind of feverish pleasure, and said to himself: "It spreads gloriously! Splendidly! There, now, that house, too, on the right will certainly catch fire! — certainly!"

Fire has something revolutionary in it: it scoffs at property — it levels the ranks of society. The *valet-de-chambre* felt this instinctively.

Within half an hour, the horizon was veiled in smoke, red below, and black above. That day the Lefort quarter was entirely destroyed by the flames. This was the beginning of that incendiarism which continued during five months. We will speak more about it anon.

At last, W. came. He was in a very good humour, and told me about the fire, which he had just passed in his carriage. Whilst speaking about general matters, he said, "that it was kindled on purpose", and added, half in jest: "yes, that reminds us of

Pugatscheff. You will see, we shall not escape either; we shall be put to the torture."

"Before they torture us", said I, "it is to be feared that they will put us in chains. Do you know that N. was arrested last night by the police?"

"By the police? you don't say so!"

"I have come on that account to you. Something must be done. Go yourself to the Prince; try to learn all about it; and obtain for me the permission to see him."

As I received no answer, I looked at W.; but in his place there seemed to stand his eldest brother. His face was distorted; the features convulsed; he kept sighing and groaning.

"What is the matter with you?"

"Have I not always told you; have I not repeated incessantly what all this must lead to? Yes, yes, this was to be foreseen; and I — I who am as innocent as a child, shall perhaps also have to suffer for it. There's no jesting about such things. I know what the casemates signify."

"Will you drive to the Prince?"

"To the Prince! In the name of Heaven, for what purpose? My advice as a friend is, that you remain absolutely quiet, that you do not even allude to N.'s fate, or it will be the worse for you. You don't know how dangerous those affairs are. I repeat it most urgently — keep aloof from that business. Whatever you do, it will be of no use to N.; you will only be caught in the trap yourself. There you see what autocracy is. Where is justice? Where is protection? Have we faithful counsel, and honest judges?"

For once I was not disposed to listen to his frivolous opinions, his caustic judgment. I took my hat, and drove away.

At home I found everything in the greatest confusion. My father was already angry with me on account of N.'s arrest. The senator had already been there with all his dignity, and had ransacked my books, laid aside those which seemed dangerous to him, and seemed much displeased.

Upon my table I found a note from General Orloff with an invitation to dinner. Might he not be able to do something? Although the attempt at W.'s had been a lesson to me, still one more effort could not do any harm.

Michael Fedorovitch Orloff was one of the founders of the celebrated Confederation of Welfare; and he was not indebted to himself for not being in Siberia, but to his brother, who was a particular friend of Nicholas, and the first who, on the 14th of December, hastened with his horse-guards, to defend the Winter Palace. Orloff was banished to his estates; and after the lapse of some years, permission was given to him to reside at Moscow. During his retired life in the country, he occupied himself with chemistry and political economy. When I met him for the first time, he conversed with me about the new chemical nomenclature.

In all energetic persons, who only at a later period of life devote themselves to a science, there springs up a particular inclination to change the order of things, and to arrange everything in a new way after their own notions. His nomenclature was far more complicated than the generally adopted French one. I wished to fix his attention, and began to prove to him in the way of a *captatio benevolentiae* that, although his nomenclature was good, still the old one was better. Orloff argued for some moments, and then gave way. My artifice had been successful, and from that time we had frequent intercourse with him. He saw in me a rising intellect; I saw in him a veteran of our opinions, a friend of our heroes, a noble apparition in our life.

Poor Orloff resembled a caged lion; on every side, he dashed his head against the iron bars. He saw nowhere a possibility of satisfying his longing for action; and this torment quite destroyed him.

Since the downfall of France, I have more than once met with people of this sort, people, namely, whose irresistible yearning for political activity made life within the four walls of their room, or still more, a domestic life, a burden to them. Such people do not understand how to live alone; solitude gives them the spleen; they begin to quarrel with their best friends, see everywhere intrigues directed against themselves, and begin at last to form intrigues of their own in order to catch some one; and by these means discover something which never existed.

Such people require a stage and spectators. On the stage they are real heroes, and will endure the utmost frowns of fortune. They want noise, thunder, disturbance; they like to be orators, to hear the opposition of their enemies. The feverish agitation of struggle and danger is an unavoidable necessity for them. Without this incentive, they fall into melancholy and sadness; they pine, decay, would like to destroy themselves, and then commit errors. Such a man is Ledru Rollin, who, a-propos, externally resembles Orloff, especially since he has let his beard grow.

Orloff's exterior was very imposing — a tall and noble figure, handsome manly features, the forehead bald, and all harmoniously proportioned, gave to his appearance an irresistible charm. He was a contrast to Yermoloff, whose wrinkled, quadrangular forehead, overshadowed by a quantity of grey hair, and his piercing look, imparted to him the beauty of a warrior who has grown old in the battle-field — the same beauty by which Mazeppa won the beauty of Marie Kotschubei.

Orloff felt so much *ennui* that he did not know how to occupy himself. He tried everything. First he established a glass manufactory, where he had windows painted after the models of the middle ages. These windows, however, cost him more than he gained by them. Another time he applied himself to writing "on credit". Nothing of all this quite suited his taste, but there was no other issue left. The lion, who dared not even give a free course to his speech, was condemned to wander about in idleness. It was a saddening spectacle to see what pains he took to make himself a learned man, a theorist.

He had a sparkling, clear, but in no way, a speculative mind. In consequence of this, he got bewildered in different newly-invented systems of well-known subjects, like the nomenclature of chemistry. Anything abstract failed entirely with him; yet, in spite of his concentrated bitterness at his ill-success, he occupied himself incessantly with metaphysics. Imprudent and reckless in his expressions, he continually exposed himself to attack. Governed by his first impressions, which were always generous and bold, he suddenly remembered his own situation, and then drew back half way. He was as unsuccessful in these political manoeuvres as with the nomenclature and metaphysics. And when he tried to amend a fault, he continually fell into a number of new ones. Hence he was constantly ridiculed. People generally judge so very superficially: they attach more importance to words than deeds, and give a greater attention to isolated faults than to the whole character.

How can such men in this country be accused from the rigorous point of view of a Regulus? It is only society which ought to be accused — that society, where no higher feeling can be displayed, but must be kept in concealment, like a contraband article, behind locked doors; and if, by mistake, a word has been too loudly spoken, every one immediately thinks, "Will not the police soon be here?"

There was a large dinner-party. I sat beside General Rajefsky, Orloff's brother-in-law. Rajefsky was likewise in disgrace since the 14th of December. Being the son of the renowned Nicholas Rajefsky, he fought, though only fourteen years of age, together with his brother, near Borodino, by his father's side. He died afterwards of his wounds, in the Caucasus. I spoke to him about N., and asked, could and would Orloff do anything for him?

A cloud passed over Rajefsky's brow; but it was not that expression of mean self-preservation, which I had seen in the morning; it was the expression of a mixed feeling of painful recollections and bitter disgust.

"The desire to help cannot be doubted here", said he; "but I question whether Orloff will be able to effect anything. Go into the study after dinner; I will tell him to join you there. Then your turn has likewise come", he added, after a pause; "this whirlpool will carry away everything."

Orloff, after having questioned me, wrote a letter to Prince Galitzin, and sought for an interview.

"The prince", said he, "is an honest man; and if he is not able to do anything, at least he will speak the truth."

The following day, I went to hear the answer. Prince Galitzin sent me a message, that N. was arrested by an imperial order; that a Committee of Enquiry had already been appointed; that the principal cause of the arrest was a supper-party on the 24th of June, at which revolutionary songs had been sung. I understood nothing of all this. This very day had been my father's saint's day. I had been at home the whole day, and N. had been with us.

I left Orloff with a heavy heart. He also was dispirited; when I gave him my hand, he stood up, embraced me, pressed me firmly to his broad chest, and kissed me, as if he feared that we were parting for a long time.

From that day, I have only seen him once, six years later. He was then sinking rapidly. I was astonished at the sick, melancholy expression of his sharpened features. He was low-spirited, and felt his decline; he also knew the bad state of his affairs, and saw no mode of extrication. Nearly two months afterwards he died. The blood was curdled in his reins.

At Lucerne, there is a beautiful monument by Thorwaldsen, cut in the savage rock. It represents a dying lion, lying in a cave. He is mortally wounded; blood flows from the wound, in which the point of an arrow is still to be seen. His mighty head rests on his claws; his breast heaves; his look expresses severe pain. All around is a desert — below is a lake. All this is surrounded by mountains, half covered with trees and grass, so that passers-by scarcely imagine that the royal animal can be there.

Once, when I sat a long while before this stone image of suffering, I recollected my last interview with Orloff.

When I went home from Orloff's, I passed the house of the Chief Officer of Police. It suddenly occurred to me to ask him candidly for an interview with N..

Until then, I had never been to any of the police. I had to wait a long time. At last, the chief officer came.

My request astonished him.

"What motive induces you to ask such a favour?"

"N. is related to me."

"Related to you?" he exclaimed, and stared at me.

I did not answer, but, likewise, stared at his Excellency.

"I cannot allow it", he said. "Your relation is *au secret*. I am very sorry."

This uncertainty — this inactivity, was killing me. Nearly all my friends were absent; it was not possible to glean any tidings. As for myself, the police seemed to have forgotten or overlooked me. It was very wearisome.

But when the whole sky seemed covered with dark clouds, and the long nights of imprisonment and exile were approaching, then a bright beam fell upon me.

Some words of deep sympathy from a young girl of sixteen years, whom, until then, I had taken for a mere child, quite moved me.

For the first time, a female figure appears in my tale. There is only one female apparition in my whole life. All other images have disappeared before her like shadows; even all the pure, youthful emotions of the heart have passed like a mist, and like the wan images of a dream; new ones have not arisen.

We met each other in the church-yard. She leaned against a monument, and spoke about N.; and my grief was appeased.

"Till tomorrow", she said, and offered me her hand. She smiled with tears in her eyes.

"Till tomorrow", I repeated; and my eyes followed her form, until she was lost in the distance.

It was the 19th of July, 1834.

CHAPTER II

The Arrest — The Police Office — The Patriarchal Tribunal

"Till tomorrow", I repeated, whilst falling asleep. I was uncommonly cheerful and contented.

Towards two o'clock in the morning, my father's valet-de-chambre awoke me. He was only half dressed, and seemed very anxious.

"An officer wants to speak to you."

"What sort of officer?"

"I don't know."

"Well then, I know", said I, as I threw my robe-de-chambre on my shoulders.

In the door-way of the saloon stood a figure wrapped in a soldier's cloak; white plumes were to be seen before the window; in the back-ground were several other figures. I recognized the cap of a Cossack.

It was the Director of Police, Müller, with his escort.

He told me that he was obliged to search my papers, by an order he held in his hands, which was written by the Governor-general. Lights were brought in. The police-officer took my keys; the Commissioner and his assistant began to ransack books, linen — every thing. The Director of Police himself commenced to examine the papers; each seemed an object of suspicion to him. He put everything aside, and, turning suddenly towards me, he said: "I must request you to dress. You will drive with me."

"Where to?" I asked.

"To the next police-office", he replied, in a tranquillizing tone.

"And from there?"

"The Governor's order contains nothing more."

I dressed myself.

Meanwhile, the frightened servants had awakened my mother. She hastened from her bed-room to mine, and was arrested at the door by a Cossack. She screamed aloud; I, frightened, hastened to her. The Director of Police left the papers, and followed me to the saloon; he apologised to my mother, made room for her, reprimanded the Cossack, although he was not at all to blame, and returned to the papers.

Then came also my father. He was pale, but endeavoured to perform his part with calmness. The whole scene began to be painful to me. My mother sat in a corner and wept. My father conversed of indifferent things with the Director of Police; but his voice trembled. I was afraid that I could not stand this much longer, and still I would not give the Commissioner the pleasure of seeing me overcome.

I therefore gave him a hint that we should depart.

"Come, come", he said, with visible satisfaction.

My father went out of the room, and returned in a moment. He brought a small image of a saint, fastened it round my neck, and said, "that his dying father had blessed him with it." I was moved. This pious present showed me the anxiety and emotion of the old man. I knelt when he hung it round my neck. He raised me up, and gave me his blessing.

The image represented the head of St. John the Baptist on a charger. What did this mean? Was it to be an example, a warning, or a prophecy? I don't know; but I was puzzled with the signification of the image.

My mother was nearly senseless. All the household servants accompanied me downstairs, surrounded me, kissed my hands. It was as if I, while still alive, were present at my own burial. The Director of Police frowned, and hurried our departure.

When we stepped out of the door, he assembled his army. With him were four Cossacks, two commissioners, and two policemen.

"Will you now allow me to go home?" asked a man with a beard, who sat before the door.

"Go!" answered Müller.

"Who is that man?" I asked, as I stepped into the carriage.

"That is the juryman; you know that unless he is present, the police cannot enter a house."

"And on that account you left him outside the door?"

"A mere formality, the poor man has lost his sleep for no purpose", observed Müller.

We drove off, accompanied by two Cossacks on horseback.

At the police office, there was no particular room for me. The Director of Police ordered me to be conducted to the Chancery, there to remain till morning. He led me there in person, threw himself in an arm-chair, yawned and murmured,

"Devil take the service! Since three o'clock on my legs like an old post-horse, and then the affair with you till the dawn of day; it is now four o'clock, and at nine I must be ready with the report. Good night", he added, after some minutes, and went away.

The policeman locked the door, and observed that, if I wanted anything I might knock.

I opened the window; the day was dawning; I felt the morning breeze. I asked the sub-officer for water, and drank a can-full. As to sleeping, it was not to be thought of.

Moreover, there was nothing whereon to lie down; except some dirty leathern chairs and an arm-chair; there was nothing in the Chancery but a large table covered with papers, and a small table in a corner, still more overladen.

The miserable night-lamp did not light the room, but only threw a glimmering ray upon the ceiling, which grew paler and paler before the approaching daylight.

I sat down in the chief commissioner's seat, and took the nearest paper from the table. It was a card of permission for the burial of a serf servant of Prince Gagarin, and with it a medical testimony that he had died according to all the rules of science. I took up another paper, it was a statute of the police; I looked through it, and found an article in which it was said, "Every prisoner has a right to learn the reason of his arrest, after the lapse of three days, or to be set at liberty."

I noticed this especially.

About half an hour later, I saw through the window our butler coming in a carriage, with a cushion, a blanket, and a cloak for me. He asked the policeman something, probably permission to see me; he was an old grey-headed man; I had been godfather to two or three children of his when still a child myself. His request was briefly and rudely refused by the Director of Police; one of our coachmen stood beside the old butler. I saluted them from the window. The Director of Police was annoyed, and ordered them to go away. The old servant bowed to the ground and wept. The coachman took off his hat, wiped his eyes, then the carriage drove away. My eyes also overflowed with tears; my heart was full; they were the first and the last tears I shed during the whole time of my imprisonment.

In the morning, the Chancery became gradually filled. First arrived the secretary, who was still intoxicated from the previous evening. This red-haired and contemptible-looking creature, covered with an eruption, represented a personification of personified dissoluteness. He wore a brick-coloured dress-coat, badly sewed, and shining with dirt at the elbows. He was followed by another person in a sub-officer's cloak. The latter was very impudent in his manner, and turned to me with this question:

"Did this happen to you in the theatre?"

"I was arrested at home."

"By Fedor Iwanowitch himself?"

"Who is Fedor Iwanowitch?"

"Colonel Müller, at your service."

"Yes, it was he himself."

"Ah! of course."

He made a sign to the red-haired officer, who, however, did not evince the least sympathy. The conversation ceased, for when the cantonist saw that I was arrested neither on account of drunkenness nor any riotous affair, he lost all interest in me, or perhaps was afraid to associate with a dangerous prisoner.

Later, some more commissioners arrived; some half asleep, and some very sleepy. At last there came several people with petitions and plaints.

The hostess of a disreputable house complained of a publican for having offended her openly in his shop by expressions which she, as a woman, could not repeat in the presence of her superiors. The publican swore he had never used such terms. The woman confirmed by an oath her statement, that he had repeatedly uttered the expressions complained of at the top of his lungs; and she added that he had lifted up his hand against her, so that, if she had not avoided the blow, her face would have been cut to pieces. The beer-seller answered, first, that she had not paid him; secondly, that she had insulted him in his own shop; and that even all this would have been nothing, but that she had threatened to have him beaten to death by her bullies.

This big, dirty woman, with half extinguished eyes, kept crying aloud in a piercing, shrieking voice; the publican expressed himself more by pantomimic jests than by words.

Instead of giving judgment, the commissioner, a second Solomon, rated both of them severely: "Too much meat", he said, "makes the dogs mad; such wretches as you should be quiet, the more so as we connive at you. What an important affair! they have been abusing each other, and then immediately come to trouble their superiors. And you, what a fine lady you pretend to be — as if you had never been insulted before; why, your business is not to be named without expressing an insult."

The publican rubbed his hands with pleasure; his face expressed the utmost satisfaction. But his turn came instantly; the Commissioner likewise addressed him: "And thou, rascal! why dost thou howl like a dog in thy shop? Darest thou abuse other people, and even lift up thy hand against them? Hast thou forgotten the hot birch rods?"

This scene had all the charm of novelty for me, and has for ever been impressed upon my memory, as the first example I ever witnessed of a patriarchal Russian process.

The hostess of the disreputable house, and the publican continued their howlings, until at last the chief magistrate entered. This latter, without enquiring why those people were present, roared at them in a still rougher voice: "Away from here! out with you! What do you take this place to be? a public-house, or a bagnio?"

When the mob had left, he turned to the commissioner, "Are you not ashamed to allow such things? How often have I repeated that the court will be dishonoured by these proceedings, and such rabble rout as that will make a Sodom and Gomorrah of it. Who is that person?" he asked, pointing to me.

"A prisoner, whom Fedor Iwanowitch has brought", the commissioner answered. "Here is also a paper, Sir."

The chief magistrate looked the paper over, and glanced at me; but when he met my firm, immovable look, fixed upon him with the intention of paying him back in kind, should he venture to address me impertinently, he said:

"I beg your pardon."

The affair between the woman and the publican once more became the object of my occupation. She wished to take an oath — the priest came, and very likely both swore. I did not see the end of the scene. I was led to the Chief Director of Police, I know not why, as no word was spoken to me; then they led me again to the police-office, where a room had been prepared for me, just beneath the watch-tower. Here the policeman observed to me that, if I desired to eat, I ought to send and buy something; for the government ration was not yet delivered, and would not be so for two or three days; and besides, this ration consisted only of three or four silver kopecks, which the better sort of prisoners generally did not claim.

It was already noontime. I sank exhausted on a dirty sofa, which stood near the wall, and fell in a sleep as deep as death. When I awoke, my mind had become quite composed. For some time, I had been so much tormented by uncertainty about N.'s fete. Now my own turn had come; danger threatened no longer from afar; it was compassing me round about. The tempest was above our heads; this first attack was our initiation.

CHAPTER III

The Watch-tower — The Lisbon
Commissioner — The Incendiaries

If a man has any internal resources at all, he very soon becomes accustomed to prison life; to the silence and perfect freedom, within his cage. There are no cares — no distractions.

At first, no books were granted. The Chief Commissioner assured me that I should not be allowed any brought from home. I begged him to buy some for me.

"It must be something instructive, then", he said. " Would you like any grammars, or things of that sort? Those would be admissible; otherwise, the General's permission must be obtained."

The proposition to read grammar to distract ennui had in it something very comical; nevertheless, I accepted it without demur, and begged the Chief Commissioner to buy for me an Italian grammar, and a dictionary. I had two red bank notes in my purse. I gave him one of them, and he immediately sent a messenger to buy the books. He gave him also a letter I had written, to forward to the Chief Director of Police, to whom it was directed, requesting him to tell me the cause of my arrest; or to set me free, according to the article which I had read.

The Chief Commissioner, in whose presence I had written the letter, tried to persuade me not to send it.

"It is useless", he said. "You will trouble the General for nothing. He will only say that you are troublesome people, and perhaps you will aggravate your case."

In the evening, the Commissioner came and said, "that the Chief Director of Police had ordered him to tell me by word of mouth, that I should learn the cause of my arrest in due time." He then produced from his pocket an Italian grammar, besmeared with grease, and added, smilingly, "By a happy chance, a dictionary has been found here, so we need not buy one expressly."

The money which he ought to have returned was not mentioned. I thought I would write once more to the Minister of Police; but the idea of acting a Hampden in miniature, in a Russian prison, seemed too ridiculous.

Ten days later, at ten o'clock in the evening, appeared a little dark-haired, pockmarked, commissioner. He brought me an order to dress and appear before the Committee of Enquiry.

Whilst I was dressing, a comic, and at the same time unpleasant occurrence took place. My family were in the habit of sending my dinner to me from home. My servant gave it to the inspector on duty; the latter sent it in to me by a soldier. Wine was also allowed, from half to a whole bottle daily. One of my friends had profited by this permission to send me a bottle of excellent "Johannisberger". The soldier and I had succeeded, by means of two nails, in taking out the cork. The bouquet was delightful, even at a distance, and I hoped to regale myself for three or four days with this wine.

It is necessary to have been in prison for some time, to become aware how much of childishness remains in the human heart, and how much pleasure may be occasioned even by a bottle of wine, or by a trick played on the guard. The pock-marked Commissioner discovered my bottle, and asked me if I would allow him to drink some of the contents. I was very much vexed, but answered, "With much pleasure." A wine-glass was not at hand; so, this monster took a large beer-glass, filled it to the brim, and poured it down his throat at one pull, without taking breath. (This way of pouring down wine, or spirits, is only to be found amongst the Russians and the Poles. No European understands what may be called swallowing his glass.) The pock-marked Commissioner wiped his lips with his blue tobacco-reeking handkerchief; and, as if to make the loss of the wine still more annoying to me, thanked me, and said, "That Madeira is not bad." I looked at him with a feeling of hatred, and felt glad that he had not been vaccinated, so that nature had not spared him.

This connoisseur of wine conducted me to the house of the Chief Director of Police, on the Twer Boulevard, and, after leading me to a saloon, left me alone. In half-an-hour a stout man entered, with an expression half lazy and half kind. He threw his portfolio on a chair, and gave a commission to the gendarmes who stood at the door.

"I suppose you are here on account of N.'s affair, and the other young people?"

I nodded assent.

"I have heard some rumours about it", he continued. "A strange and incomprehensible affair."

"I have now been a prisoner for more than a fortnight on account of this affair; and not only do I not understand it, but I absolutely know nothing of it."

"That is all right", he said, looking fixedly at me. "You must not know anything of it. Excuse me giving you a bit of advice. You are young; your blood is hot; you would easily grow angry, and that would be unlucky. Therefore, mind, you must not know anything of it; that is the only means of safety."

I looked at him with astonishment. His face betrayed no evil meaning. He guessed my thoughts, and said, smiling, "I was myself a student at the Moscow University twelve years ago."

Hereupon, an officer entered, to whom the stout gentleman gave several orders, and then left the room, nodding kindly with his head, and putting his fingers on his lip. I never again met this unknown person; but I have experienced the soundness of his advice.

Next the Director of Police came. It was not Fedor Iwanowitch, but another, who made me appear before the Police Commission.

In a spacious and handsome saloon, five persons were seated round a table; all in uniform, with the exception of one decrepid old man. They were smoking cigars, and conversing merrily; their uniforms were unbuttoned, and they had thrown themselves back without much ceremony in their armchairs. The Chief Director of Police presided; and when I entered the saloon, he turned round to a creature, and addressed him with the words: "Father, if you please!"

I now first noticed the person addressed. It was an old priest, with a grey beard, and a violet-coloured face, who sat in the corner. He was slumbering, and would certainly rather have gone home; he was thinking of other things. He yawned, and covered his mouth with his hand. In a somewhat drawling and nasal voice, he began to exhort me; spoke about the sin of concealing truth from persons who are "installed in their office by the Emperor; and about the uselessness of such concealment, considering the omniscient eye of God. He did not even omit to refer to different Biblical texts — as, for example: "There is no power save of God", and "render unto Caesar the things that are Caesar's", and so on.

When he had finished, he desired me to kiss the Bible, and the beatifying Cross in confirmation of my vow to confess the truth. But I had never taken this vow; it was not even asked for.

When he had finished, he hastily covered up the book and cross. Zinsky, the Chief Director of Police, told him he might now go, and scarcely rose from his chair to salute him.

He then turned to me, and translated the spiritual speech into the official dialect.

"I will add but one thing to the words of the priest", he said; "you have not the possibility of denying, even if you liked to do so"; and he pointed to a quantity of papers, letters, and papers, which were purposely spread on the table.

"Only a sincere avowal can mitigate your fate, and it depends upon yourself, either to be set at liberty, or to be sent to Bobruisk or the Caucasus."

The questions were put in writing. The naiveness of some of them was remarkable.

"Are you acquainted with any secret association?"

"Did you not belong to such a one, a literary one or otherwise?"

"Who are the members?"

"Where do they meet?"

It was easy for me to answer all these questions in the negative.

"I see you know nothing", said Zinsky, looking over my answers. "I have warned you, you will only aggravate your position by it."

So ended the first hearing.

Eight years later, the other wing of that house was inhabited by a lady who had herself been very handsome when young, and had a beautiful daughter. She was the sister to the new Director of Police.

Every time, when I visited her, I passed the room where Zinsky had examined us. At that time, and even later, there was the portrait of the Emperor Paul on the wall of this saloon. Was it in order to remind us how low man may sink by dissoluteness and abuse of power; or was it to encourage the police to barbarity? I know not, but there it was, with the characteristic flat nose, the wrinkles in his face, and the stick in the hand of the despot. Once, when a prisoner, later, as a guest, each time I passed, I stood still before that portrait. The small adjoining saloon, where an air of feminine grace and beauty presided over everything, seemed to be established by mistake in this house of police and judgment, and I always felt sorry to see such a beautiful flower growing within the stone walls of a police court-house.

The conversation, which was restricted to a small circle, frequently assembling in the saloon of the ladies, was full of irony, and astonished the ear, accustomed to hear within those walls nothing but trials, accusations, reports about domiciliary visits, and such things. The same walls which then separated us from the whispering of the commissaries, from the noise of the entrance and exit of prisoners, and the clanking spurs and swords of the Oural Cossacks.

Some weeks later, the pock-marked commissioner came again and conducted me once more to Zinsky. In the hall several men, in chains, were lying or sitting, surrounded by armed soldiers. In the first room were likewise several persons of different ranks, strongly guarded, but not in chains. These were the incendiaries; Zinsky was present at the fire; we must await his return.

We entered at ten o'clock in the evening, and at one, I was still sitting quietly in the ante-room, in the company of the incendiaries. At length, one, and then another of them was called; the policeman ran to and fro; the chains rattled; the soldiers went through their exercise, to chase away their ennui. At last, Zinsky arrived, covered with ashes and soot; he ran hastily into his cabinet; nearly half an hour later my commissioner was called, he returned very pale, his face was convulsively distorted. Zinsky thrust his head through the door and said, "Monsieur Herzen, the whole commission has waited for you this evening; that blockhead brought you hither, whilst you had been sent for by Prince Galitzin. I am very sorry that you have waited here such a long time; but it is not my fault. What is to be done with such subalterns? I believe he has been fifty years in the service, and still remains a donkey. Now set off, and go home!" he said, in a still harsher voice.

During the whole way, the Commissioner repeated: "Good Heavens! what a misfortune! no man knows or dreams what may happen to him; now he will ruin me. It would have been of no consequence if they had not waited for you at the prince's, but that was a great fault. Good Heaven's what a misfortune!"

I pardoned him the "Rhenish", and the more so when he confessed to me that he felt now much more anxiety than he had done once at Lisbon, where he was in danger of being drowned. This last circumstance was so unexpected to me, that I could not help laughing.

"What in all the world took you to Lisbon?" I asked.

The old man had been in the navy five-and-twenty years before. It is not to be denied that the minister was right, when he assured Captain Kopekin in Gogol's dead souls, that no service remains unrewarded in Russia.

The old man Fate had spared in Lisbon, in order that he should be scolded here by Zinsky, like a school-boy, after forty years service, and, after all, he was not in the wrong.

The commissioners named for the inquiry by the chief governor displeased the Emperor; he had a new one formed under the direction of Prince Galitzin, who had been sent for that purpose from St. Petersburg, Zinsky, Schulensky, colonel of the Gendarmes, and the former Auditor Oransky. In the order of the Chief Director of Police, it was not stated that the place of meeting for the commission had been changed; therefore, it was quite natural that the Lisbon Commissioner should have conducted me to Zinsky.

At the police-office there was likewise a great excitement. This evening, not only had fires broken out at three different places, but messages had been sent there twice by the Commission, in order to learn what had happened to me, or whether I had escaped. The poor Lisbon man had again to bear his share of reproaches and scornful words from the Chief Commissioner, who was in the wrong himself, by not having asked expressly where I was to be taken to. Upon a couple of chairs in the corner of the Chancery, lay a man groaning fearfully. I turned to him, and saw he was young and fine-looking, well dressed, and apparently suffering dreadfully, and spitting blood. The physician of police advised him to be taken as early as possible in the morning to an hospital.

When the policeman had led me again to my room, I tried to learn from him the story of the wounded man. He was a retired officer of the guards, who had had an intrigue with a femme-de-chambre, and was paying her a visit at the moment when the house was fired. The incendiaries had for some time caused a fearful alarm, and, indeed, not a day passed without the alarm-bell being heard twice or thrice. From my window, I saw each night the sky - coloured by the reflection of the flames, as if by the rising sun. The officer, in order not to compromise the girl by his presence, when the house caught fire, escaped over a hedge, and hid himself in a stable-loft of an adjoining house, to wait for a moment favourable for escape. But a little girl in the court-yard had seen him, and told the first policeman who hurried up, that one of the incendiaries had hidden himself in the loft. Several policemen rushed into it, followed by a great many of the mob, and triumphantly dragged the officer out. He was so unmercifully beaten and ill-treated, that he died on the following morning.

An attempt was now made to classify the prisoners; one half were set at liberty, the other half declared suspected. The Director of Police came every morning to examine them. These examinations lasted three or four hours, and were often accompanied by floggings and blows. The lamentable cries and whining, the complaints and entreaties of the women, together with the sharp, threatening voice of the Director of Police, and the monotonous reading of the secretaries reached my ears. It was dreadful — unendurable! These sounds pursued me in my dreams; I awoke, and shuddered at the idea that these unhappy beings, with their bleeding, lacerated backs, were lying a few paces from me, in chains, and upon straw, and doubtless, they were innocent.

In order to form an idea of a Russian prison, of Russian jurisdiction, and Russian police, a person must be either a peasant, a menial servant, workman or citizen. The political prisoners are certainly severely treated, and cruelly punished, but their fate can in no way be compared with that of the poor bearded men. The latter are treated without ceremony, and to whom should they address their complaints? Where can they find justice?

The disorder, the brutality and arbitrariness of Russian courts of justice, and Russian police, are of such a nature, that the poor man fears his punishment less than the preceding process, and awaits with impatience the moment of his departure to Siberia, as a deliverance. His torments terminate where his punishment begins. And it must not be forgotten, that three parts of those, imprisoned upon a mere suspicion, and declared innocent afterwards by the Tribunal, have to go through the same torment as those who are guilty.

Peter III. abolished the Secret Chancery and Torture-room.

Catherine II. abolished torture.

Alexander I. abolished it a second time.

Answers extorted by brutality are not valid before law. Any official who tortures an accused man is himself subject to the most rigid punishment.

And yet, notwithstanding all this, people are tortured through the whole of Russia, from Bering's Straits to Tauroggen. Where blows are not allowed, other means are resorted to, and prisoners are made to endure insupportable heat, thirst, salted food, and other atrocities. For instance, one man was put on an iron floor with bare feet at ten degrees of cold; he fell ill, and died some time afterwards in an hospital, which was under the superintendence of Prince M. who himself related this case with indignation.

The superiors know all this; the governors hush it up; the governing senate connives at it; the ministers are silent, the emperor, the synod, the landed proprietors, down to the commissioners are all united herein, and agree with Leligshaw.[4] "Why not beat the peasant a little, for the peasant must at times be curbed."

The commission, nominated for the examination of the incendiaries sate (that is to say, beat them) for six long months, though without any result. The Emperor grew angry, and ordered the affair to be wound up in three days. It was so. Guilty people were of course found and condemned to the knout, to being branded, and to forced labour; the menial servants were summoned from every house to behold this dreadful execution of the incendiaries. The winter was already far advanced. I was in prison in the Krutin Barracks. A captain of the gendarmes, a good old man, who had been present at the execution told me the particulars of it.

The first of those condemned to the knout, turned to the people, and said in a loud voice that he was innocent, and did not know what he had spoken under the influence of pain. Here he took off his shirt and exclaimed: "True believers, look here!"

One scream of horror burst from the multitude; his back was all one huge, blue wound, and upon this wound the knout was again to play.

The murmurs and the gloomy looks of the assembled people induced the police to make baste. Several executioners gave the number of blows decreed, others branded, while others chained the prisoners' feet together, and the affair seemed terminated.

---

[4] A character in one of Gogol's novels.

But the scene had so surprised the inhabitants of Moscow, that it was spoken of in all the different circles. The chief governor made a report of this to the Emperor; the latter ordered them to examine anew the case of the incendiaries, who protested against the punishment. Some months later, I read in the newspaper, that the Emperor had granted the sum of two hundred roubles banco, as a compensation for each blow, to two innocent men who had been punished, and had ordered that they should receive a special pass in which their innocence was testified, despite of their being branded. These two were the supposed incendiary, who had addressed the people, and one of his friends.

The fire in Moscow, in the year 1834, which was repeated ten years later in several provinces, remained an enigma. That it was kindled on purpose there is no doubt. In general, incendiarism is a very common means of revenge with us. We continually hear of conflagrations; at one moment the house of a nobleman is burnt down; then a corn magazine, and so on. But the reason of the frequent fires in Moscow, in the year 1834, was not discovered by any one, and least of all by the Commission.

Before the 22nd of August, the Coronation Day, papers were found dispersed in many places, in which the inhabitants were told that they need not trouble themselves about the illumination; that it would be provided without their aid.

This circumstance occasioned anxiety and inquietude to the timorous magistrates of Moscow. The Police Office was filled from morning till night with soldiers. In the court-yard stood a squadron of Ulans. In the evening, patrols on horseback and on foot were seen perambulating the streets incessantly. In the exercising school, the artillery was in readiness. The police officers ran to and fro along the streets with Cossacks and gendarmes; even Prince Galitzin rode through the town with his adjutants. This warlike appearance of the peaceful city of Moscow was unusual, and had an effect upon the nerves. I was at my window, beneath the watch-tower, till late at night, and watched the manoeuvres in the court-yard. The Ulans had camped themselves in troops around their horses; others were mounted. The officers went round with an air of importance, and cast contemptuous glances on the police officials. The Town Adjutants came riding up in their yellow collars, looked very anxious, and went off without having done anything. This night no conflagration took place.

Soon afterwards, the Emperor himself came to Moscow. He was discontented with everything and everybody; with the Commission, with our being tried by the General, and not by the Secret Police, and with the non-discovery of the incendiaries. In a word, we soon felt the presence of the "Most High".

CHAPTER IV

The Krutin Barracks — Tales of the Gendarmes — The Officers

Three days after the arrival of the Emperor, late in the evening (such matters as these are done during the darkness, in order not to disturb the public) a police-officer brought me the order to pack up my things and follow him.

"Where?" I asked.

"You will see", he answered, prudently and politely.

It may be supposed that I did not continue the conversation, after such an answer, but took up my things, and followed him.

We were a long while on our way. At last, after a drive of nearly an hour and a half, we passed the Simonoff Monastery, and stopped at a massive stone door, guarded by two gendarmes with carbines. This door led to the former Krutin Monastery, which has now been converted into a gendarmerie barrack.

I was taken to a small office. The secretaries, the adjutants, the officers, all wore blue. The officer on duty, in full uniform and helmet, asked me to wait a little, and even invited me to smoke my pipe, which I held in my hand. Then he signed a receipt for the delivery of the prisoner, gave it to the commissioner, went out, and returned with another officer, who said to me:

"Your room is ready; have the goodness to come."

A gendarme lighted us. We went down stairs, crossed the court-yard in a few steps, and then went through a small door into a long corridor, lighted by a solitary lantern, and with small doors on either side. One of these doors led into a guard-room of most limited dimensions, behind which was a cold, damp, pestilential little room, into which the officer with the shoulder-knot invited me to enter; adding in French, that "he was *désolé d'être dans la nécessité* of examining my pockets; but that he could not help it, as military rules demanded obedience, &c."

After this polite preamble, he turned very simply to the gendarmes, and directed a glance towards me. Forthwith, one of the latter plunged an enormously great and rough list into my pocket. I said to the well-bred officer, "that such strong measures were entirely superfluous, for I would empty my pockets myself; but, after all, what could they possibly contain after an imprisonment of six weeks?"

"We are quite aware of that", said the officer with the shoulder-knot, with a self-complacent smile. "But we also know the order of the division of police." The officer on duty smiled, likewise, slyly.

But the gendarme was ordered to continue his search, and I emptied my pockets myself.

"Pour out your tobacco on the table", said the officer who had been désolé.

I had a pencil and a pen-knife in my tobacco-pouch, enveloped in paper. I thought of them from the first, and, whilst speaking with the officer, I had played with the tobacco-pouch, until the knife came into my hand; then I boldly poured the tobacco on the table, holding the knife with the pouch. The gendarme returned the tobacco to the pouch — my knife and pencil were saved. This might have been a lesson for the officer with the shoulder-knot, for having made such contemptuous remarks about the division of police.

This little event put me in a very good humour, and I began to examine my new domain with fresh spirits.

The cells of the monks — built three hundred years before, and half sunk into the ground — had been converted into worldly cells for political criminals. Mine contained nothing but a bed without a mattress, one chair, and a small table, whereupon stood a jug with water, and a large copper candlestick, in which a thin tallow candle was burning. The cold and damp made me tremble; the officer ordered the store to be lighted, and went his way. The soldier had promised to bring me some straw. Meanwhile, I lay down on the bare bed, with my cloak under my head, and smoked my pipe. In a few minutes, I observed the ceiling of the cell was covered with innumerable wood-lice

(*Blada Germanica*). They had not seen any light for a long while, and now came from all sides towards the glare of the candle, swarmed about, pushed each other, fell on the table, and then ran, like mad, round its edges. I never liked wood-lice, nor, in general, any of those unbidden guests. These co-partners of my cell were truly disgusting to me; still, I would not complain, and submitted to the trial.

Three days afterwards, however, the insects retired to the soldier, on the other side of the wall, where it was much warmer; only now and then one or so came up, poked its head in, and then returned quickly to warm itself.

Although I had entreated the gendarme not to shut the stove, after having lighted the fire, he did it nevertheless. Through the heat, I felt very unwell — my brain swam — I tried to get up to call the soldier, and really arose, but forthwith fell senseless.

When I recovered, I found myself stretched on the floor with a violent headache. Before me stood an old grey-headed gendarme, with folded hands, looking at me with staring eyes quite void of expression; just as in certain groups of bronze, the dog looks at the turtle.

"Well, you have had it a little too much", he said. "Here is horseradish, with salt and kvas. I have already let you smell it, and now I'll give you some to drink."

I drank; he raised me, and laid me on my bed. I felt very ill; the window could not be opened; the soldier went into the office, to ask if he might take me into the open air in the court-yard; but the officer on duty replied: "He could not allow it on his own responsibility, and neither the Colonel nor the Adjutant was in the way." Thus I was obliged to remain in the hot room.

By and bye I, too, became accustomed to the Krutin Barracks, conjugated Italian verbs, and read all sorts of books. At first, we were treated severely. At nine o'clock in the evening, at the last roll-call, the soldier came in, extinguished the light, and locked the door. I had to sit in darkness from nine o'clock in the evening till eight in the morning! I never was a heavy sleeper, and particularly not in prison. Without any exercise, few hours of sleep were more than sufficient. What a punishment, then, to have no light! Add to this the cries of the watch, repeated at every quarter of an hour, calling out "Sluschai!" in a loud and long-sustained key, on both sides of the corridor.

Some weeks later, Colonel Simonoff (brother of the famous actress), allowed the calls of the watch to be suspended, and candles to be introduced, on condition that the window, which was lower than the court-yard, should have no curtain, so that the guard could see everything that the prisoner did. A little later, we were granted an inkstand by the governor, together with permission to walk in the yard. Paper was given us, on condition that the sheets should be counted, and remain entire. We were allowed to walk once a day, accompanied by the officer on duty, and by a soldier, in the yard, which was surrounded by a ditch, and a line of gendarmes on duty.

Life passed on monotonously and quietly, and acquired from its military uniformity a mechanical and regular character like the caesura in poetry. In the morning, with the assistance of the soldier, I boiled my coffee on the stove; at ten o'clock the officer on duty made his appearance, and brought in with him, I know not how many cubic inches of cold air. He was dressed in cloak, helmet, and gloves, had tremendous shoulder-knots, and rattled his sword as he moved. At one o'clock, the gendarme brought a dirty table napkin, and a dish of soup, which he held by the rim, so that his thumb was perceptibly cleaner than his other fingers. The food was tolerable; but it must not be forgotten that it cost me two roubles banco daily, which, in the course of nine month's imprisonment amounted to a rather considerable sum for a man without a fortune.

The father of a prisoner once declared that he had no money. He was coldly answered that in that case it must be stopped from his pay. Very likely he would have been imprisoned if he had had no pay to receive.

I must observe here, also, that Colonel Simonoff received daily thirty-five kopecks of public money for the sustenance of each prisoner. The thing began to make some noise, but was hushed up, as the adjutants, who profited by the stolen money, appeased the whole division of gendarmes by giving them tickets for the best performances at the theatre. The evening tattoo was followed by a deep silence, which was interrupted neither by the crackling steps of the soldiers on the frozen snow, nor by the signal of the watches. I generally read until two o'clock in the morning, and then extinguished the light. Dreams sometimes carried me off into liberty, and awakening still half asleep, I thought, "My God! what a gloomy dream — prison! gendarmes!" and my heart was overjoyed that all was but a dream, when —lo! all at once a sword rattled in the corridor, and an officer, accompanied by a soldier with a lantern in his hand, opened the door, or the cry of the watch, "Who goes there?" or still worse, the shrill sound of the trumpet close beneath my window, pierced the morning air.

In the tedious, solitary hours, when I was tired of reading, I gossiped with the soldiers who watched me, especially with the old man who had saved me from suffocation. All the old people are released from active service as a particular favour, and consigned to the quiet life of gaolers. They stood under the command of a sergeant — that is to say, a spy and a rogue. The whole service was performed by five or six gendarmes. The old one, of whom I speak, was a good and simple creature, grateful for the slightest kindness, which, very likely he had rarely experienced in his life. He had been in the campaign of 1812; his breast was covered with medals. His time of service was over, and still he remained in service, because he did not know what else to do.

"I have written home twice to the Mohileff provice", he informed me; "but I have received no answer. It seems that none of my relations are still alive; and it is hard, in one's old days to be reduced to beggary."

The individuality of a man is sacrificed unscrupulously by us without the least compensation.

Such a gloomy character pervaded the old man's tales, that he always made me thoughtful.

In the year 1817, he had been in the campaign against the Turks, under the command of a very kind-hearted captain, who took care of all his soldiers, as though they were his children, and in fact was always at their head under fire.

"A Moldavian woman", Philimonoff related, "had bewitched the captain. We observed once that he was very distressed. The thing was, look'ye, that — you understand — he had remarked that the Moldavian went also to another officer. He then called us one day, me and one of my comrades, a fine fellow, both whose legs were shot off later at Little Jaroslav, and told us how the Moldavian had betrayed him, and asked if we would assist to give her a lesson for it.

'Why not,' we answered, 'we are always ready with all our heart to serve your Lordship.'

He thanked us and said, 'she will certainly go this night to see him (showing the house where the officer lived) post yourselves on the bridge, and when she passes, grasp her silently, and into the river with her.'

'Very well, Captain,' we said. We provided ourselves with a sack and sat down on the bridge; towards midnight the Moldavian came. We went up to her. 'Where are you going in such haste, gracious lady?' we exclaimed, and with these words, she received a blow on the head. The sweet heart did not utter a sound; we put her into the sack, and threw her into the water. The following day our captain went to the officer and said, 'don't be angry with the Moldavian girl; we slightly prevented her coming; that is to say, she is just now lying at the bottom of the river. But I should like to take a little walk with you, with swords or pistols, which ever you prefer.'

Well then, they had a duel. Our Captain was shot through the chest, the good man pined away, and some months after he expired."

"And the Moldavian?" I asked, "was she drowned?"

"She was drowned", the soldier observed.

I observed with astonishment the child-like carelessness with which the old gendarme told me this story, and he, as if he now reflected about and understood it for the first time, added, as if to tranquillize me, and to appease his conscience, "she was but a heathen, such people were just the same as if they were unbaptised."

The gendarmes always received, on each Imperial holiday, a glass of brandy. Philimonoff used to omit drawing his brandy for five or six times in succession, that he might have five or six glasses at once. He marked the number of the glasses he had not received on a piece of wood, and on the most solemn festivals, he went and fetched them. He poured this mass of brandy into a soup dish, strewed crumbs of bread into it, and ate this breakfast with a spoon; he then smoked a large pipe with a very small stem; his tobacco was uncommonly strong, he used to cut it up himself, and called it sagaciously — "selbst-hack". Whilst he smoked, he curled himself up like a worm, on a small window-sill, a chair was not to be found in the guard's room, and sang:

"The girls came to the meadow,
Full of grass and flowers."

And the more his intoxication increased, the more the words altered; flowers, lowers, owers, were and then he fell asleep. But what robust health he must have had; he was above sixty; had been wounded twice, and was still able to bear such a breakfast!

Before I leave these Flemish barrack pictures, *á la Wouvermann*, and these prison tales, which resemble the recollections of all prisoners, I will say some words about the officers.

They were, for the most part, very good fellows, not spies, and only by chance in the division of gendarmes; young nobles without fortune, as they had learned little or nothing at all, they had become gendarmes because they could find no other employment. They performed their duties with military accuracy, but I saw not the least zeal in any one of them except in the adjutants; but that was just what had procured for them their posts. When I became better known to these officers, they facilitated, as far as was in their power, my obtaining of many little comforts, and it would be wrong to complain of them.

A young officer told me that in the year 1831, he was ordered to arrest a Polish land proprietor, who was accused of being in communication with the revolutionary emissaries, and said to be hidden in the neighbourhood of his country seat. After the proper inquiries had been made, he went to the place where the proprietor of the estate was said to be, surrounded the house with his detachment, and entered it with two gendarmes; the house was deserted; they went through all the rooms, searched every corner, but nobody was to be found. Still, many little things showed that the house had been recently inhabited.

The officer left both the gendarmes down stairs, and went once more to the very top of the house. He searched most carefully, and found, at last, a small door which led to a store-room; the door was locked from within; the officer pushed it with his foot, it gave way, and a tall and beautiful woman stood before him. She pointed silently to a man who held a girl of about twelve years of age, nearly insensible in his arms. It was the man they sought for and his family. The officer was confused. The noble looking woman observed this, and said:

"Can you be cruel enough to ruin them?"

He stammered some excuses, uttered some of the commonplace phrases about duty and unconditional obedience, and at last quite in despair, seeing that his words had not the least effect, said:

"What shall I do?"

The lady looked proudly at him and answered, pointing to the door:

"Go down, and say that nobody is here."

"I don't know what became of me, and how it happened", continued the officer, "but I went down, and left the house with my soldiers; two hours later we were searching most zealously for the proprietor of the estate at another place. He is said to have afterwards escaped, and crossed the frontier. That was a woman!"

Nothing in the world is more inhumane or imprudent than wholesale judgments passed on actions in the abstract, considered merely by appearances. Jean Paul Richter has very justly observed: "When a child has told a lie, tell him that he has lied; but don't tell him that he is a liar, otherwise you would ruin his moral confidence." If we are told, "That is a murderer", we immediately expect to see a hidden dagger, a brutish expression, which conceals dark purposes, as if murdering was the usual occupation, the trade of a man, who has perhaps once in his life killed somebody.

It is impossible to be a spy, or executioner, to be a trader in vice, and, at the same time, to be an honest man; but it is possible to be an officer of the "gendarmes", and not to have lost all human dignity, just as we often find amongst those unhappy victims of social corruption, gentleness, generosity, and female delicacy. I have a dislike to those people who do not understand, or will not take the trouble to understand what is beneath the surface of things, who cannot account for a crime or an unhappy complicated situation, but instantly either very wisely pass a summary sentence upon the affair, or coldly turn away from it; that is the common way of dealing with actions, of abstract, dry, egoistic natures, who are disgusting in their purity, or of poor, trivial souls who have never been tried, and have never undergone a serious temptation. These are, in fact, at home on that filthy ground where the others have only tripped.

CHAPTER V

The examination — Galitzin, Senior — Galitzin, Junior — General Staal — The Sentence — Sokolofsky

But, meanwhile, how did it go on with our affair with the trial?

Before the new Commission, the business did not progress quicker than before the old one. The police had observed us for a long while, but they were too impatient, in their zeal, to wait till they could have found out a palpable ground of accusation. They sent us an officer in disguise, Skaretka, to induce us to betray ourselves. He became acquainted with all of us; but we soon guessed his intentions, and kept him at a distance. Some other young people, chiefly students, were not so circumspect; but they had no serious intercourse with us.

A student, after having terminated his course of studies, gave a dinner to his friends on the 24th of June, 1834. Not only were none of us present, but none were even invited. The young people became intoxicated, had a good deal of fun, danced Mazurkas, and, amongst other things, sang in chorus the following song of Sokolofsky's:

> "The Emperor's gone to join
> The Heavenly congregation,
> And forms a charming subject
> For anatomization.
> The empire and the nation
> For him begin to whine;
> To govern them then hastens
> The monster Constantine.
> But to the mighty Tsar,
> The lord of Earth and Heaven,
> The Russian Tsar departed,
> Hath a petition given.
> God read, and then revealed,
> His mercy all divine,
> For Nicholas He gave us,
> That king among the swine!"

In the evening, Skaretka suddenly remembered that it was the day of his patron saint He told a story about his having sold a horse very advantageously, invited all the students to come with him, and promised a dozen bottles of champagne. All went; the champagne appeared, and the host, already somewhat unsteady on his legs, proposed a repetition of Sokolofsky's song. Whilst they were singing, the door was opened; Zinsky, with some policemen, entered.

All that was stupidly, rudely, and awkwardly managed. The police wished, at any rate, to hold us tight; at the same time they sought for an apparent reason, in order to entangle, by the same opportunity, five or six other persons for whom they were on the watch; and instead of these they seized twenty innocent ones.

But the Russian police is not easily to be disconcerted. Two weeks later, we were arrested for having taken part in the festival. At Sokolofsky's, they had found letters from N. M., at M. M.'s, letters from N., and at the house of this latter, mine; but in spite of all that, they discovered nothing. The first examination entirely failed.

To make the second one more successful, the Emperor sent the most distinguished of Inquisitors, A. T. Galitzin, from Petersburg.

This race is rather rare with us; belonging to it were the well-known chiefs of the third division (that is, the Secret Police) Mordwinoff, the rector Pelikan, of Wilna, some employees, from the Baltic provinces, and some corrupted Poles.

But, most unfortunately for the Inquisition, the Commandant of Moscow, Staal, was named first member of it. Staal, an honourable warrior, an old and brave general, examined the case, and found that it had two different sides, possessing nothing in common. Namely, on the one side, a festival which required a police punishment, and on the other the arrest of some people imprisoned — Lord knows why, and whom it would-be difficult, as well as ridiculous, to condemn for some half-uttered opinions.

Staal's opinion did not please the younger Galitzin. The contest between the two assumed a very decisive character. The old warrior flew into a passion, struck his sword against the table, and said, "instead of ruining men, you should rather make the proposal to close the universities; then, at least, other unhappy victims would be spared. But after all, you may do what you like, only without me. I will never again enter the meeting place of the Commission." With these words, the old man hastily left the saloon.

All this was reported on the very same day to the Emperor, and on the following, when the Commandant appeared before him, the Emperor asked him, why he would not go any more to the Commission? Staal told him everything.

"What nonsense!" said the Emperor, interrupting, "to quarrel with Galitzin What a shame! I hope you will continue to visit the Commission as you have done hitherto."

"My Emperor:" answered Steal, "spare my grey hairs, I have grown grey without having ever deserved blame. My zeal is known to your Majesty. My blood, the last days of my life belong to you, but here my honour is in question — my conscience revolts against what is going on in the Commission."

The Emperor's countenance changed, Staal bowed, and appeared no more at the Commission.

This anecdote, the truth of which is undoubted, throws a clear light upon the character of Nicholas. How was it, that it did not occur to him that the affair could not be quite right, when a man like Staal, a brave and well-deserving veteran, from whom even he could not withhold his esteem, refused to take a part in it, because he thought it incompatible with his honour? The least he ought to have done was to summon Galitzin, and to let Staal explain the affairs in his presence. He did nothing of the kind, but ordered us, on the contrary, to be treated more severely.

After that, there remained in the Commission none but enemies of the prisoners, under the chief command of an old simpleton, who, after the lapse of nine months, knew as little of the affair as nine months before. He always maintained a pompous silence, assumed a mien of the utmost importance, took but little part in the conversation, and merely asked, at the end of each examination, "Can we let him go?"

"Yes", answered Galitzin, junior, and Galitzin, senior, would remark with emphasis, "you may go."

My first examination lasted four hours — the questions were of two kinds. The first were put for the purpose of discovering the opinions opposed to the spirit of the government, and the sentiments developed by the "pernicious reading of St. Simonian works", as Galitzin, junior, and the Auditor, Oransky, expressed themselves.

These questions would have been extremely simple, had they been questions at all. Our opinions were expressed plainly enough in the papers and letters seized. The material fact of our having written such lines or not, was the only object left for inquiry. The Commission thought it necessary to add to each plainly written phrase, "how do you explain the following sentences of your letter?"

There was nothing to explain, and I answered with some rhetorical phrases.

The Auditor had discovered in one letter, the following sentence: "All constitutional charters lead to nothing. They are nothing but mere contracts between the master and his slaves; the task is not to ameliorate the condition of the slaves, but to prevent the existence of slavery."

When I was summoned to explain this sentence, I said that, "I saw no necessity for defending a constitutional form of government, and were I to do so, it might be made a charge against me."

"The constitutional form of government can be attacked from two different sides", observed Galitzin, junior, with his nervous shrieking voice. "You do not attack it from the monarchical point of view, else you would not speak of slaves."

"Then I commit the same fault as the Empress Catherine, who ordered her subjects never to call themselves slaves."

Galitzin, junior, nearly suffocating with rage at this ironical answer, said,

"You surely don't imagine that we are assembled here to fight out scholastic differences. Do you think that you are defending a thesis in the university."

"Why do you ask for an explanation?"

"You feign not to know what is asked of you."

"I really do not know."

"What an obstinacy in them all!" observed the President.

Galitzin, junior, shrugged his shoulders, glanced at the Colonel of the Gendarmes, Schubensky, and smiled.

"Exactly like N." added the President, giving me, by that, a notice about my friends.

A pause ensued. The commission always assembled in the library of Prince Galitzin. I turned round to the book-cases, and looked at the books. Amongst others, there was a many volumed edition of the works of St. Simon.

"What injustice!" I said to the President. "I am under an accusation on account of St. Simon's writings; and in your library, Prince, there are more than twenty volumes of his works."

As the good old gentleman had never read anything since he was born, he did not know what to answer. But Galitzin, junior, looked at me with his basilisk eyes, and asked:

"Are you blind, that you don't see that these are the writings of that St. Simon who lived in the time of Louis XIV?"

The President smiled, looked at me, and nodded, as if to imply, "Ha! my friend, hast thou also been mistaken for once?" — and said, "Go!"

When at the door, I heard him ask: "Is this the person who has written what you showed me about Peter the First?"

"Yes, it is", answered Shubensky.

I lingered a moment.

"He has talent", observed the President.

"So much the worse. In skilful hands, poison is only the more dangerous", added the inquisitor. "That is an incorrigible, pernicious young man."

These words were my sentence.

Here is a counterpart to St. Simon.

When the police-officer searched N's papers and books, he laid aside one volume of the "History of the French Revolution", by Thiers; then a second, then a third, then a fourth, and so on. At last, his patience failed, and he said: "Good heavens! what a mass of revolutionary books! And there is another!" he added, giving to the Commissioner, Cuvier's address "sur les révolutions du globe terrestre."

The other category of questions was much more complicated. All kinds of police tricks and artificial means, usual at trials, were employed to catch us in a trap, and entangle us in contradictions. Hints were given about the confessions of our other friends, and various moral tortures of a similar kind. It is not worth the trouble to relate them, only that they did not succeed in making us contradict the others, so that they could have confronted us.

After the last question had been put to me, I sat alone in a room where we used to write the answers. All at once, the door was opened, and Galitzin, junior, with a sad and thoughtful expression of countenance, entered.

"I have come", he said, "to speak to you before the end of your trial The acquaintance my deceased father had with yours for many years, inspires me with a particular interest for you. You are young, and you can still have a brilliant career; but, to enable you to do it, you must get out of this affair, and fortunately that depends on yourself. Your father has been deeply affected by your arrest, and now lives in hope to see you free again. We have just now been speaking about it with Prince Galitzin, and we are sincerely disposed to do all that is possible, if you will give us the means to save you."

I understood the meaning of these words. The blood rushed to my cheeks. I bit my pen with anger.

He continued: "You are going straight to the casemates, or under the white strap. You will send your father into the grave by your conduct. He will not survive the moment when he sees you in the grey soldier's cloak."

I was about to answer him, but he interrupted me.

"I know what you are going to say; but stop a moment. It is evident that you had views against the Government. In order to make it possible for us to implore the pardon of the monarch, we must have proofs of your repentance. You are obstinately silent; you evade answering. You spare, through a false sense of honour, people of whom we know more than you do, and who have not been so discreet as you. You will not help them, but they will ruin you. Write a letter to the Commission, simple and sincere; confess that you are convicted of your error — that you have been led astray, owing to your youth — and name the unhappy ones who are the cause of it. Will you purchase your own future happiness, and the life of your father, at this small cost?"

"I don't know anything, and will not add a single word to my explanations."

Galitzin rose, and said, in a harsh tone: "You will not? Well, it is not our fault."

This closed the trial.

In January or February, 1835, I was, for the last time, summoned before the Commission. I was summoned to read my answers through, to alter them if I liked, and to sign them. Schubensky alone was present. When I had finished reading, I said to him:

"I wished to know how you can accuse a man from these questions and answers? Under which paragraph of the code shall I be placed?"

"The code is destined for crimes of another kind", answered the Colonel of the "Blues".

"That is another thing; but when I read these literary productions, it seems to me impossible that this can be the whole cause for which I have been in prison during seven months."

"And do you really think", interrupted Schubensky, "that we believe you, and that we don't know that you had formed a secret society?"

"But where is that society?" I asked.

"It is your good luck that the traces of it have not been found out; that you have not yet had time to begin operations. We have prevented you in time; that is to say, we have saved you."

Whilst I signed my declarations, Schubensky rang the bell, and ordered the priest to be called. The priest came, and certified beneath my signature that all my avowals had been made voluntarily, without the least constraint. It must be understood that he had never been present at the examination, and that, not even for appearance sake, had he ever asked me a single question. A counterpart to the sworn juryman behind the door!

From this time, our confinement became a little less severe. Our nearest relatives could obtain permission to see us. In this way, two other months passed away.

Towards the middle of the month of March, our sentence was pronounced. Nobody knew what it was. Somebody said that we should be sent to the Caucasus; others, that we would be taken to Bobruisk, and others again hoped that we would be set at liberty. This last was Staal's opinion, who also expressed it to the Emperor. He suggested that the time during which we had been imprisoned, should be considered our punishment.

At last, we were all ordered to appear before Prince Galitzin to hear our sentence. This day was to us the greatest of festivals. Here we saw each other again for the first time, since our imprisonment.

With loud and joyful acclamations, we embraced each other, and shook hands, surrounded by a circle of military and gendarme officers. The meeting revived us all; there was no end to the tales and anecdotes.

Sokolofsky was also amongst the number; somewhat pale and thin, but, nevertheless, in the full brilliancy of his wit.

He, the author of "The Creation", "Chever", and some other very good poems, was gifted by nature with a rich vein of invention;

but he was not so wildly independent as to be able to dispense with the developments of civilization, while his mind was not cultivated enough to develop itself independently. He was a noble man, who looked at the world with a poet's eye; but he was no politician. He was amiable, entertaining, a good companion in merry hours, a "bon vivant", fond of drinking and dash, as we all were, perhaps a little more. He was above thirty years of age. His works were in fashion at the time; they were well paid for, but he had never a penny in his pocket; within four and twenty hours he always spent what he got. Taken to a prison from a feast by accident, Sokolofsky behaved exceedingly well; his mind was elevated in prison. The auditor of the commission, a pedant and pietist, who had grown grey and lean through envy and covetousness, asked Sokolofsky, apparently through respect for the throne and altar, and as if not understanding the grammatical sense of the last two verses:

"To whom do you apply the detestable words at the end of your poem?"

"Be assured", answered Sokolofsky, "that they do not apply to the Emperor, but to God. I direct your attention particularly to this extenuating circumstance."

The auditor shrugged his shoulders, looked up to the ceiling, then regarded Sokolofsky for a long while silently, and finally took a pinch of snuff.

Sokolofsky had been treated worse than the rest; he had been put in a state prison, in solitary confinement, in a dark cell, and, nevertheless, as I have said, he was of a good cheer, and animated us by his anecdotes.

Galitzin made his appearance in *grande tenue* with a blue ribbon; then came Zinsky in the household uniform. The Auditor, Oransky, had put on a sort of civil military frock of light green, in order to celebrate this day of joy. The commandant, of course, did not come.

The noise and laughing, however, had so much increased during that time, that the Auditor entered the saloon with threats, and said: "That these loud conversations and this laughing, were a dreadful proof of our contempt for the sovereign's will, which we were about to hear."

The door was opened. The officers divided us into three sections; in the first were Sokolofsky, Utkin, a painter, and Ibayeff, an officer. We were in the second; the third were *tutti frutti*.

The sentence was specially read to the first section; it was of unheard of atrocity. The accusation was based upon high treason. The accused were ordered to Schüsselburg for an undefined time. All three listened to this horrible sentence with heroic composure. Utkin died two years afterwards in the casemates. Sokolofsky was — already half dead — sent to the Caucasus, and died at Piatigorsk. After the death of the two first, a residue of shame and conscience induced the government to transport the third to Perm. Ibayeff did in his own fashion, he became a mystic.

Utkin, "a free artist confined in prison", as he described himself at the trial, was a man of about forty years. He had never taken any part in political affairs; but noble-minded and impetuous as he was, he had given free course to his tongue before the commission, and had spoken sharply and roughly towards its members. In reward, they tortured him to death in a damp casemate, where the water oozed from the walls.

Ibayeff was more guilty than the others, because he wore epaulettes. Had he not been an officer, he would not have been so severely punished. This poor man had participated, by chance, in a revelry, and had very likely drunk and sung; but certainly neither more, nor more loudly than the rest.

Our turn then came. Oransky wiped his spectacles, hem'd, and began the edifying lecture of the supreme decision. Its contents were as follows: — That the Emperor, after having read the report of the Commission, and in consideration of the youth of the criminals, commanded that we should not be handed over to the court of justice, but that we should be informed that, although, according to law, people who had committed high treason by the singing of revolutionary songs, were to be punished with death; and that this punishment, according to other laws, could only be mitigated into life-long labour in a house of correction — yet this most gracious Emperor pardoned most of the criminals, and permitted them to live at their own homes, under the surveillance of the police. Those more severely incriminated were subjected to such punishments as would lead to their rehabilitation. These punishments were: — sending them off to distant provinces for an undefined time; or admitting them into the service of the state, under the surveillance of the local magistrates, &c.

There were six of these latter. The first name was mine! I was destined for Perm. Amongst the six thus punished was Lachtin, who had never been arrested. When he was called before the Commission to hear his sentence, he thought they were only trying to frighten him, by showing him how the others were punished. It was said that some one of Galitzin's suite had a pique against Latchin's wife, and, therefore, had prepared this surprise for him. He was of a delicate health, and died in the third year of his exile.

When Oransky had terminated his lecture, Colonel Schubensky appeared on the stage. With selected words, and in a style *á la Lomonosoff*, he announced to us that we were indebted for the grace of the Emperor to the generous President of the Commission. Schubensky expected that all of us would thank the prince after these words. But it happened otherwise, only a few of those pardoned bowed, whilst glancing furtively at us. But we stood with folded arms, without the least sign of emotion at this imperial and princely favour.

Then Schubensky took another tack to obtain his aim, and said to N., "You are bound to Pensa, do you think that happened by chance? In Pensa, your father is prostrated by a stroke of apoplexy. The Prince has asked the Emperor to send you to this place, in order to soften somewhat by your presence, the pain occasioned to him by your exile. Is it possible, then, that you don't find sufficient reason to thank the Prince?"

There was no help; N. was obliged to bow. This was what they wished to obtain.

The old Prince was satisfied, and now, I don't know why, called next on me. I stepped forward with the firm intention of not thanking him, whatever he or Schubensky might say; and the more so, as he sent me to the most distant and the most disagreeable, town.

"You go to Perm", said the Prince. I was silent.

The Prince was confused, and, in order to say something more, he added, "I have an estate there."

"Do you wish me to take a message to your steward?" I asked smilingly.

"I give no commissions to people like you — to Carbonari."

"What do you want of me, then?"

"Nothing."

"I thought you called me."

"You may go", interrupted Schubensky. "Permit me, Colonel", said I, "as I am once here, to remind you of your words, the last time we met at the commission. I was not accused by any one of having taken a part in the festival, and yet in my sentence, I am said to be one of the guilty. There must be some misunderstanding."

"Do you mean to protest against the supreme will", said Schubensky, "take care that Perm do not change into something worse. I will write down your words."

"That was just what I was about asking you to do. It is said in the sentence: 'according to the report of the commission.' I answer to that report, and not to the supreme will. The Prince is my witness that I have not even been questioned about the festival and the songs."

Schubensky, becoming pale with rage, said, "As if you did not know that your guilt is ten times greater than that of those who were present at the festival. There stands one", pointing to one of the pardoned, "who has, in a state of drunkenness, been seduced to join in an abominable song; however, he afterwards begged pardon on his knees, and with tears in his eyes. But you are far even from repentance."

The person whom the Colonel had thus exposed, was silent. He neither replied, nor did he die of shame; but the lesson was a good one. Such is the usual result of dirty actions.

"I beg your pardon", I continued, "it is not the question here, whether my guilt is great or little; but if I am a murderer, I will not be regarded as a thief. I will not allow it to be said — even with the intention of excusing me — that I, as you expressed yourself just now, had committed this or that offence in a state of intoxication."

"If I had a son, an only son, so cunning, I would ask the Emperor myself to send him to Siberia", said Schubensky.

The chief director of police now interposed with some nonsense. It was a pity that the younger Galitzin was not present; it would have been an opportunity for a display of his rhetorical powers.

All this ended, of course, in nothing.

Lachtin approached the prince and asked to have his departure delayed:

"My wife is near her confinement", he said.

"That is no fault of mine", answered Galitzin.

Mad dogs, when they bite, have at least an earnest appearance; but this half-witted aristocrat, who enjoyed moreover the renown of being a kind-hearted man.

*****

In spite of the repeated warnings of the police and gendarmes' officers, we once more remained together in the saloon for a quarter of an hour, embraced each other, and took leave for a long time. With the exception of Obolensky, I saw none of them again till my return from Wiatka.

Our departure was imminent.

Our former life in prison was continued during the interval. Our departure for the desert terminated it.

The friendly meetings of our youthful days were at an end. Our exile would last, certainly, for some years; where and when should we meet again — should we meet again at all?

I regretted my former life, and parting from it so suddenly without taking leave. I dared not even hope to see N.. In the last days, two of my friends had succeeded in obtaining an interview with me, but that was not sufficient for my heart.

To see once more my young comforter, to press her hand as I pressed it in the churchyard; that was what I longed for. With a glance at her eyes, I would bid farewell to the past, and go to meet the future.

We did see each other for some minutes, the 9th of April, 1839. It was in the evening. The following morning, I departed.

For a long time afterwards, I kept that day in my memory as a festal one; it contained one of the happiest moments of my life.

Why, then, do such terrible recollections arise when I think of this day, and of all the bright days of my past existence? A tomb — a crown of dark red roses — two children, whom I held in my arms — torches — a multitude of exiles — moonlight — the ocean at the base of the mountains — an address which I hardly understood, and which, however, lacerated my heart — all is past!

CHAPTER VI

Exile — The Police-Master at Pokrov — The Wolga — Perm

On the 10th of April, in the morning, an officer of gendarmes took me to the house of the Governor-General. In a secret division of his office, my relations were allowed to take leave of me.

But, of course, the meeting could not be very agreeable at such a place. Spies and secretaries — the reading of instructions for the gendarme who was to accompany me — the impossibility of saying a word without hearers — in short, a more offensive and unpleasant position could hardly be conceived. I breathed again freely, when at last my carriage rolling along the borders of the river Wladimika.

> "Per me si va nella citta dolente;
> Per me si va nel eterno dolore."

I wrote down those two verses of Dante at one of the stations, as they are as well adapted for the road to Siberia as for the entrance into hell.

Seven wersts (one mile) from Moscow is an inn, called "Peroff". One of my most intimate friends had promised to wait there for me. I proposed to the soldier, who guarded me, to drink a glass of brandy — he consented; it was far from the city. We went in; but my friend was not there. I lingered in the inn as long as I could possibly find excuses for so doing, till the soldier would not wait any longer; the coachman began urging his horses, when, lo! a troika (light carriage, drawn by three horses) came hurrying on direct towards the inn. I rushed to the door. Two strangers — merchant's sons on a pleasure trip — sprang noisily from the telega. I gazed wildly at the distance — not one moving point — not one single person was to be seen on the road to Moscow. It was hard to drive on. I gave twenty kopecks to the coachman, and we flew off like lightning.

We drove on without stopping. The gendarme was ordered to travel not less than two hundred wersts (twenty-eight miles) in twenty-four hours. That would have been moderate, were it not in the beginning of April; the road was partly covered with ice — partly with mud and water — and became more and more impracticable, the nearer we approached Siberia.

The first event of the journey happened in Poktowa. We had lost several hours on account of the ice, which interrupted the communication between the two shores of the river. The gendarme was, therefore, in great haste, but the postmaster declared that he had no horses. The gendarme showed him the passport giving him authority to demand courier horses, when there were no post-horses. The postmaster excused himself, by saying that all the horses were taken for the Private Secretary to the Minister for the Home Affairs. But when my gendarme began to talk big, the postmaster ran away, in order to get fresh horses from the inhabitants of the place. The gendarme went with him. I was annoyed at remaining alone in the dirty room of the postmaster's house, and therefore went out, and began to walk up and down before the house. This was my first walk, without being accompanied by a soldier, after an imprisonment of nine months.

When I had thus walked nearly half-an-hour, a man in a military coat without epaulettes, and with a blue ribbon, *pour le mérite*, round his neck, came up to me. He looked at me with persevering impudence, went past, came back again, and asked in an impertinent manner:

"Is it you whom the gendarme is conducting to Perm?"

"It is", I answered, without stopping.

"But, I beg your pardon, how dare he then?"

"With whom have I the honour to speak?"

"I am the chief of the police", the stranger answered; and his tone betrayed a deep consciousness of his dignity. "I am expecting the arrival at every moment of the Minister's Private Secretary; and, behold! political prisoners are walking unguarded in the streets. What a blockhead that gendarme must be!"

"Will you have the kindness to make your observations to him?"

"I will not make observations to him, but have him arrested, and sentenced to a hundred lashes; and have you taken off by a policeman."

I did not wait the termination of his speech, but proceeded with quickened steps to the post-house. I heard him through the window, raging, and threatening the gendarme. This latter excused himself, but did not seem very much frightened. After some minutes, both entered the room. I sat facing the window, and did not look at them. By the questions which the chief of police addressed to the gendarme, I saw immediately, that he was dying of curiosity to know why I was exiled, and all about it. I persevered in remaining silent. The chief of police began a speech, addressed neither to the soldier nor me.

"Nobody can justly appreciate our situation. Can it be agreeable to me to quarrel with a soldier, or to inflict inconvenience on a man I never saw before in my life? Every responsibility weighs upon the Chief of Police; he is the responsible landlord of the whole town. Whatever may happen, he will be told, 'Answer for it.' Has the Government cash-box been robbed? — 'Thou art guilty.' Is a church burnt down? — 'Thou art guilty.' Are many drunken people in the streets? — 'Thou art guilty' If they drink little wine? — 'Thou art guilty, likewise.'

He was very much pleased himself with this last observation, and continued, in a gayer tone:

"It is lucky, notwithstanding, that you met me; for, if you had happened to meet the Minister, and passed him in the same way, he would have exclaimed: 'What! a political prisoner! The chief of police must be summoned before a court of justice.' "

Weary of his fine speech, I turned round to him and said:

"Do as you like, but I only beg that you will spare me your remarks. I see by your words that you expected me to bow to you. I am not accustomed to bow to those I do not know."

The chief of police grew confused. It is always so in our country; the man who first makes a noise, or begins a row, gets the upper hand. If a person speaks with a superior, and allows him once to raise his voice, all is lost; for, if he hears his own voice, he becomes a wild beast. But if you roar at him at the first gross word, he gets frightened and will certainly yield; he is then convinced that he has to deal with a man of a firm character, and such people must not be goaded too far.

The chief of police sent the gendarme to inquire about the horses, and turned to me as if to excuse himself.

"I acted thus chiefly on account of the soldier. You don't know our soldiers; it is not possible to show the least indulgence to them; but, believe me, I can make a distinction between persons. Allow me to ask you what unhappy chance —"

"When our affair was terminated, we were forbidden to speak about it."

"Oh! in that case — of course — then I dare not —" and his look expressed the torments of unsatisfied curiosity. He was silent for a moment, and then continued, "a distant relation of mine passed a year in the fortress of Peter Paul, you understand, also on account of certain associations, and so on — but, I beg your pardon, I fear you are still angry. I am a strict military man; in my seventeenth year I entered the army. I have an impetuous temper, but a moment after all is forgotten. I will leave your gendarme in peace — the devil take him."

The gendarme re-entered with the answer that no horses could be procured for an hour.

The chief of police told him he pardoned him on account of my intercession; he then turned to me, and said:

"You will not refuse my request, I hope, as a proof that you are not angry, do come and breakfast with me. I live two doors from here; but you must come at a venture, and be satisfied with what God gives."

This proposal was so ridiculous, after our having met in such a way, that I accepted his invitation, ate his caviar and drank his Madeira and brandy. He was so exceedingly complaisant, that he told me all about his family connexions; yes, even about the illness of his wife which had lasted seven years. After breakfast, he took out of an urn, which stood upon the table, a paper, and handed it to me with visible pride and satisfaction; it contained some verses of his son's which had been read at the public examination in the cadets' school. After having given me such proofs of perfect confidence, he proceeded artfully to question me indirectly concerning my affairs. This time I satisfied him partly.

The chief of police put me in mind of a secretary to a provincial court of justice, of whom a friend once told me. Nine presidents of the court had succeeded each other, whilst this secretary unchangeably remained on his post, and always went on in the same way with his affairs.

"How do you manage", my friend asked him one day, "to agree with every one of your different superiors?"

"Well, with the help of God, I get happily through it. It is true that many of them were angry at first, raged, cried, and scolded, threatened to dismiss me, or to send me into a distant province. However, our part is a subordinate one; it is best to be silent, and to remember that, in a short time, the new superior will become as tired as the rest; he is for the first time in harness, and, in fact, before you can think of it, he gets into quiet training, and all goes on as well as you can imagine."

When we approached Kasan, the Wolga was at the full height of its tide; the passengers were obliged to travel a whole station from Ustona to Kasan on a raft, as the river had over-flowed its banks for a space of, at least, fifteen wersts. It was a stormy day, and the passage of the river was also suspended. A mass of telegas, and various carriages, were waiting on the bank.

My gendarme went to the overseer, and asked for a raft. The overseer did not like to give one, and said it would be better to wait; as it was, no one could tell what might happen from one hour to the other. But the gendarme was in haste, partly because he was drunk, partly because he wanted to show his importance.

They put my carriage upon a raft of middling size. The weather became apparently calmer. After half an hour, the boatman, a Tatar, hoisted a sail, when, all at once, the storm we had fancied appeased broke out afresh. We were carried on with such force, that we drove irresistibly against a pile, and struck so violently that our feeble raft sprung a leak, and began letting in the water.

Our situation was not agreeable; but the Tatar succeeded in bringing us to a sand bank.

A merchant ship happened to pass just then.

We called out to them, and begged them to lower a boat. The crew heard us, but went on unheeding. A peasant with his wife now approached in a small boat, and enquired what caused our situation.

"Oh, that's nothing!" said he; "only stop the hole, and then, in God's name, go forward. What is there to bother about? You, because you are a Tatar, don't know how to act." With these words, he sprang upon our raft.

The Tatar was, in fact, very much frightened, firstly, because the gendarme who had been aroused from his sleep by the rising water immediately sprang tip and began to beat him; secondly, because the raft was the property of government. He repeated incessantly, "If the raft sinks, what will become of me?" I tried to comfort him, with the assurance that, in that case, he would also perish. "Very well, little father", he answered, "if I am drowned, it is all very well; but if not?"

The peasant stopped the hole in the raft with the assistance of the rest. He hammered with his axe, nailed a plank upon it, then went up to his waist into the water, helped the others to draw the raft from the bank, and we soon found ourselves again in the current of the Wolga. The river was terribly swollen; wind and water mixed with snow beat in our faces; the cold stuck to our vitals, till we at last beheld the monument of John the Cruel looming through the mist and watery clouds. The danger seemed past, when, all at once, the Tatar cried, "It is leaking! it is leaking!" and, in fact, the water was pouring rapidly through the plugged hole. We were at the most dangerous spot; the raft moved slower and slower, and the moment of our sinking could be foreseen.

The Tatar took off his cap and began to pray. My valet-de-chambre was quite unmanned. He wept, and said repeatedly "farewell, my little mother, I shall see thee no more." The gendarme abused them all in his rage, and threatened to beat them when once again on shore.

At first, I too was alarmed; the more so as I was almost blinded by wind and rain. But the thought of how ridiculous it would be to perish there in such a way? The childish sentence "quid timeas? Caesarem vehis!" gained the upper hand, and I waited quietly, convinced that I was not to find my death between Ustona and Kasan. For this proud confidence we generally are punished later in life, and then we lose it. Hence youth is so heroic; but when a man grows older, he becomes prudent and is seldom carried away by enthusiasm.

Quite frozen, and wet to the skin, we reached the shore about a quarter of an hour afterwards, near the walls of the Kremlin of Kasan. I went into the first public-house, drank a glass of brandy, ate a hard-boiled egg, and proceeded to the post-house.

In the villages and smaller towns, the travellers always find a room for their use at the postmaster's. In the larger towns, they are obliged to alight in the hotels. I was taken to the office at the post-house. The post-master showed me his room, which was occupied by an old invalid, who was in bed, a woman and several children. There was not one unoccupied corner, where I could change my clothes. The gendarme would not take me to an hotel. I wrote to the General of the gendarmes, and requested him to allow me a room where I could warm myself, and dry my clothes.

An hour passed before the gendarme returned. He said that Count Apraxin had ordered him to let me have a room. I waited once more for two hours; nobody came. I sent the gendarme a second time. He brought the answer that Colonel Pol, to whom the general had sent the order to provide a room for me, was playing at cards in the noble club, and that no room could be provided until next day.

That was gratuitous cruelty. I wrote again to Count Apraxin, and requested him to let me continue my journey immediately, as I hoped to find a resting place at the following station. The Count was asleep, and my letter remained unopened till the next morning. There was nothing for it; so I cast off my wet clothes, wrapped myself in the cloak of my guard, and lay down on the table of the office, having, instead of a pillow, a thick book covered with linen.

In the morning, breakfast was brought. The officers began to assemble, and one of them observed to me, that it was not proper to breakfast in a magistrate's office. To them, individually, it was all the same, but the Chief of Police might be angry at it.

I answered in jest that those only could be driven away who had it in their power to go out; but whosoever did not enjoy that power, was, *nolens volens*, obliged to drink and eat where he had been imprisoned.

On the following day, Count Apraxin decided that I might stop at the hotel in Kasan for two or three days.

During that time, I wandered about the town with my gendarme. Everything here recalls Asia — the East — veiled Tatar women; the men with high cheek-bones; orthodox churches and mosques beside each other. At Wladimir, at Nijny, one feels the vicinity of Moscow; but here you are apparently far from the capital.

At Perm, I was at once conducted to the Governor. He was entertaining a large company, in celebration of his daughter's wedding with an officer. The Governor insisted on my introduction; and I was forced to present myself to the society of Perm in my soiled travelling dress, and covered with mud.

The Governor talked all sorts of nonsense; forbade me making the acquaintance of the exiled Poles; and told me to come to him in a few days, when he would give me some occupation in his office.

This Governor was from the south of Russia; did not maltreat the exiled, and was a good sort of man. He had managed quietly in his nook to better his position, burrowing like a mole; he had put aside, unobserved, one straw after the other, so that he would be taken care of in his old days.

Through an incomprehensible taste for control and order, he had ordered that all those exiled to Perm should present themselves before him every Saturday, at ten in the morning.

He then appeared himself with his pipe and a piece of paper; he counted the heads to see that all the exiles were present, and if one of them was wanting, he sent a commissioner to inquire the reason. He scarcely spoke to anybody, and then dismissed us. In this manner, I made the acquaintance, in his saloon, of nearly all the Poles against whom he had warned me.

The day of my arrival, the gendarme went back, and I found myself, for the first time since my arrest, at liberty.

At liberty! in a little town on the frontiers of Siberia, without the least experience, without knowing in any way the society in which I had to live.

From the nursery I had passed to the university, thence into the circle of my friends, where theories and reveries were discussed, but business was unknown. Then came the prison, and formed the transition to practical life, which began for me here, near the mountains of the Ural.

But I had not had time to get accustomed to this life, when the Governor announced to me that I was to go to Wiatka, because another exile, destined for Wiatka, had requested to be taken to Perm, as he had relations there. The Governor decided that I should set off on the following day. That was impossible; for believing myself destined to remain for some years in Perm, I had bought several things which I should be obliged now to sell again at half their value. After some evasive answers, he allowed mo to remain two days longer, but demanded my word of honour not to seek any opportunity for seeing the other exiles.

Next day, I was about selling my horse and different things, when the Chief of Police entered my room, and ordered me to leave the town within twenty-four hours. I explained to him that the Governor had granted me a delay. The Chief of Police shewed me a paper in which he was in fact ordered to send me off within twenty-four hours. This paper was signed by the

Governor, the very same day on which I had obtained from him the above mentioned permission.

"Very well", said the Chief of Police, "I understand it is pretty clear, our worthy master put the responsibility upon my shoulders; shall we go and see him?"

"Come."

The Count said he had forgotten the promise he had given me. Thereupon the Chief of Police asked him artfully, "whether he would not direct the order to be written again."

"That is not worth while", answered the Count, with a simple, child-like expression.

"Now we have caught him", said the Chief of Police to me, and rubbed his hands with pleasure.

The Chief of Police at Perm, belonged to the peculiar type of half civil, half military officers. These people, who by a happy chance have been thrust against a bayonet, or have been driven in the way of a bullet, receive by preference the appointments of Chiefs of Police. They accustom themselves in the army to a certain frankness, stock their memory with various phrases about the purity of honour, generosity, &c., and practise biting satires against the clerks in the civil offices. The younger men amongst them have read Marlinsky and Sagoskin, know the beginning of Pushkin's 'Caucasian Prisoner' by heart, are acquainted with Woinarofsky, and cite famed passages of verses at every opportunity. This, for instance, whenever they meet anybody smoking, they repeat the verse of Pushkin;

"Yantar v'ustach yego dimilsa" (The amber pressed between his lips).

All of them, without exception, acknowledge loudly that their position is far below their merit; that necessity only enchains them to that world of ink; that were it not for their wounds and their poverty, they would be adjutants, general, or generals of divisions in the army, each of them cites some striking instance of a former companion and says: " there are by way of illustration, Kreutz, Rüdiger — we were made ensigns at the same time, lived together, called each other Peter, John, &c, but you see £ am no German, I had no influence, and now I am vegetating here as an overseer. Believe me it is a hard thing for a noble minded man, with our views to occupy a post in the Police."

The wives of this kind of men are louder in their lamentations than the husbands; but nevertheless every year, with a sorrowful heart they invest their spare cash in the Savings' Bank of Moscow, whither they make the journey, under pretext of a sick mother or aunt, and their desire to see her once more in life. In this way they spend their fifteen years. The husband complains of the hardness of fate, beats the policemen, thrashes the citizens, cringes and bows before the governors, helps the thieves to escape, steals documents, and repeats verses of Pushkin. The wife, while complaining likewise of her fate, and of provincial life, accepts all possible presents from the inhabitants, plunders the tradesmen and petitioners, and dreams of poetry and moonlight walks.

I have lingered a little longer perhaps than I ought on these characteristics, because I was myself deceived at first by these gentlemen, taking them for somewhat better than the rest; but this is in nowise the case.

I arrived at Wiatka in three days, after having passed through entire districts inhabited by Woteks, Mordwines, and Tscheremisses.

CHAPTER VII

Wiatka — The Office and Dining-Room
of Ilia Excellency, K. S. Tufeyeff

The Governor of Wiatka did not receive me on arrival, but he directed me to be told that I might appear before him on the following morning at ten o'clock.

In the morning, I found in the reception-room the Captain of the district, the Chief of Police, and two officers. They were all standing, whispering to each other, and glancing uneasily at the door. The door opened, and an old man entered; he was not very tall, but broad-shouldered, and his head was fitted on his shoulders like a bulldog's. His projecting cheek bones completed the likeness to the dog. His hyena-like smile, his withered face, with a licentious expression, his small, piercing grey eyes, a few upstanding hairs, all this united, made an inexpressibly disgusting impression.

In the first place, he gave the Captain a sharp reprimand, on account of the road he had travelled the previous day. The man stood before him with downbent head as a proof of profound respect, and answered to all he said, as in former times servants used to do. "I hear, your excellency."

After this, the Governor turned to me with an impertinent look, and said,

"You have passed your examination at the University of Moscow."

"I am a student."

"Have you ever served in the army?"

"In the Kremlin expedition."

"Ha, ha, ha! a fine service; oh! of course, then you had plenty of time to enjoy yourself and sing songs. Alenizia", he shouted as a scrofulous-looking young man entered.

"Listen, good friend, there is a student from the Moscow University. He understands, very likely, everything except service. The Emperor wishes him to learn it with us; employ him, therefore, in the office, and give me reports about him. Tomorrow morning, at nine, you will present yourself at the office", he said, turning to me, "now you may go. But wait a little, I forgot to ask you how you write."

I did not understand at first what he meant.

"Well! your handwriting I mean."

"I have nothing about me to show it."

"Bring a pen and paper hither."

Alenizia handed me a pen.

"What shall I write?"

"Whatever you like", said the secretary. "Write, for instance, 'after the examination it was proved.' "

"Well, you won't copy reports for the Emperor", said the Governor, with a satirical smile.

I had already, at Perm, heard a great deal about Tufeyeff, but I found him surpass my expectations. What strange productions Russian life brings forth!

Tufeyeff was born in Tobolsk. His father was one of the poorest citizens, and, I believe, an exile. When a boy of thirteen, young Tufeyeff joined a wandering band of actors, who went from fair to fair in the smaller towns, dancing on the tight rope, and giving acrobatic performances. He followed them from Tobolsk to the Polish provinces, amusing the people by his antics. There he was arrested, Lord knows why, and as he had no passport, he was sent on foot as a vagabond, with a party of prisoners, to Tobolsk. His mother, who had become a widow in the meantime, lived in the greatest poverty. Her store fell to pieces, and the son was obliged to rebuild it himself. It became necessary to find some occupation for the boy. He read and wrote pretty well, and obtained the place of a clerk in the magistracy. Bold by nature, he was sharpened and well trained by his varied education, first among the acrobats, and then among the prisoners, with whom he made the journey from one end of Russia to the other.

In the beginning of Alexander's reign, an imperial commissioner arrived at Tobolsk, he wanted several secretaries, and somebody recommended young Tufeyeff. The commissioner was so satisfied with him, that he made him the offer to take him to Peters-burg. Tufeyeff, from that moment, formed another opinion of himself; until then, his ambition, as he himself said, had not gone beyond the place of a secretary in a provincial court of justice; but from this time, he valued himself higher, and resolved with an iron will to make his way.

And he did so; within ten years, we find him the indefatigable secretary of the Intendant-General Kankrin. One year later, he appears as the chief of an expedition sent by Araktjiyeff, whose ministry governed the whole of Russia. He was with this Count at Paris, when the allied troops entered it; but he was, during the whole time, immersed in the war-office, and positively did not see one single street of Paris. Day and night, he and his worthy comrade, Kleinmichel, were occupied in composing and re-writing documents.

Araktjiyeffs office so far resembled a copper mine, that the workmen could only stand the labour there for a few months, or they would have died. At last, Tufeyeff got likewise tired of this manufactory of orders and ukases, and looked out for a more quiet post.

A man like Tufeyeff, without any high pretensions, and of one plodding bias of mind, apparently honest, eaten up by ambition, and convinced that subordination was the first human virtue, would quite naturally become a favourite with Araktjiyeff. This latter rewarded him with the office of a vice-governor, and gave him, some years later, the government of Perm. Tufeyeff now saw at his feet that same province, through which he had once wandered, bound with a cord, and at another time dancing on one!

The power of a governor increases in an arithmetical progression with the distance from Petersburg; but it increases in geometrical progression in those provinces where there is no nobility, as in Perm, Wiatka, or Siberia. Just such a country suited Tufeyeff.

He lived there like an Asiatic Satrap, with this difference only, that he was active, busy, always occupied, and interfered in everything; at the same time, however, he resembled a commissioner of the Convent in the year '94, a sort of Carrier, save that his energy and hard-heartedness served autocracy instead of revolution.

His was a coarse nature; he lived a dissolute life, and suffered no opposition. His influence was exceedingly corruptive. It was said that he could not be bribed, and yet, after his death, it was found that he had accumulated a nice fortune. He was severe towards his subalterns; pursued, without indulgence, those who were detected in their peculation, and with all that, his officers stole more than ever. He abused his power beyond measure; for instance, when he gave an officer orders to examine into some affair in which he was interested, he told him, at the same time, that the affair would probably be so and so, and woe to the officer if it proved otherwise.

Perm was still full of Tufeyeffs fame. He had there a number of adherents who were hostile to the new Governor, because this latter, very naturally, had surrounded himself with people of his own party. But there were likewise people who hated him; one of these, a very original specimen of the Russian race and the Russian training system, warned me earnestly against Tufeyeff. I speak of the doctor of one of the mining establishments there. This clever and very energetic man, had, heaven knows how! soon after the termination of his studies, formed a very unhappy matrimonial engagement hereafter. He went to Yekaterinburg, and was plunged into the stagnation of provincial life without any previous experience.

Although his position in this circle was tolerably independent, still he was lost in it, and his whole activity was reduced to sarcasms about the officials. He laughed at them openly, and said to them the most offensive things, accompanied by gibes and jeers.

As nobody was spared, nobody was particularly angry at the doctor's sharp tongue. He had acquired, by his attacks, a position in society, and forced that same society, denuded of principles as it was, to submit to his never-resting rod.

I had been warned against him, and told that he was mad, and exceedingly impertinent; but with all that a very good doctor. I found his jokes and his tittle-tattle neither offensive nor dull; on the contrary, full of humour, and a refined irony. There were his poetry, his vengeance, his cry of woe, perhaps, also, the expression of his despair. He studied the circle of officers like an artist. As a physician, he knew their most insignificant and most secret passions; and, encouraged by their awkwardness and anxiousness, he permitted himself every liberty.

At every word, he used to add, "It does not cost a farthing!" Once I made, in jest, an observation on this eternal repetition.

"Why do you wonder at that?" he answered. "The aim of each speech is to convince; therefore, I am always ready to add the most convincing argument which exists in the world. Assure people that it will not cost a farthing to assassinate their own fathers, and they will do it."

He was likewise always ready to give, if any one wanted to borrow of him, small sums of forty or fifty roubles. Then he took his purse from his pocket, and asked when the debtor thought of paying him.

"Now I will bet you a silver rouble", he would say, "that you will not pay me the money at the fixed time."

"I beg your pardon, Sir, but what sort of a man do you take me for?" the other would reply.

"It costs you not a farthing", the doctor would say, "what I take you for; but the thing is this. I have kept an account that lasts six years on this very subject; and not one of my debtors has paid at the time agreed on; and scores have not paid at all."

The time passed, the doctor would ask quite seriously for the rouble he had won.

On one occasion, the farmer of a brandy distillery in Perm, was desirous of selling a travelling coach. The doctor went to him and made the following speech, without stopping once.

"You want to sell a coach; I want one; you are a wealthy man, a millionaire; therefore you are respected by the whole world; and I am come to pay you my respects. As you are a wealthy man, it must be all the same to you, whether you sell your coach or not; but I want a coach very much, and I have very little money. You will certainly overreach me, and profit by my not being able to do without a carriage; you will ask 350 roubles for it. I shall offer you 180; I shall call every day in order to bargain for it; and in about a week, you will reduce your demand to 175 or 200. Would it then not be better to begin with that?"

"Much better, indeed", answered the astonished farmer, and gave him the coach.

The day of my departure for Wiatka, he came in the morning to see me, and began:

"Your fate is like Horace's — you have sung once, and now you are continually 'translated.'"

Then he took his portfolio from his pocket, and offered me money for the journey.

I thanked him, and said that I did not want it.

"But why will you not take it? It won't cost you a farthing."

"I have money."

"That is a bad sign", he continued, when I declined it again, "the end of the world is approaching."

Then he opened his tablets, and noted in, them "for the first time, after a practice of fifteen years, I have met a man who refuses money, and who, moreover, is about to go away."

When he had done joking, he sat down on my bed, and said seriously, "you are going to a terrible man; beware of him, and keep as far as possible from him. Should he happen to like you, it would be a sad recommendation for you; should he hate you, then he will find means to subdue you by calumny, self-invented accusations, and Heaven knows what else."

He then told me a story, the truth of which I had, at a later time, the opportunity of seeing confirmed by certain documents in the office of the minister of Home Affairs.

Tufeyeff had had an intrigue with the sister of a poor employee. The brother of this girl was sneered at, and he determined to break off the connection. He threatened them with exposure, which he would transmit to St. Petersburg. In short, he annoyed them so long, that one day he was seized by the police, taken before the magistrates, that he might be declared insane.

The magistrates, the president of the police, the chief of the medical council (an old German, who was very much beloved by the people, and whom I knew personally) all agreed in pronouncing Petroffsky a lunatic.

Our doctor knew Petroffsky, and had treated him before; he was examined on the subject as a mere formality. He declared to the chief of the medical council, that Petroffsky was by no means mad, and proposed to renew the examination, else he must carry the matter further.

The magistrates were not, in the least, against this proposal; but unfortunately, Petroffsky died suddenly in the mad-house, before the second examination could take place, although he had been up to that moment in perfect health.

The affair was referred to St. Petersburg.

Mademoiselle Petroffsky was arrested. (Why not Tufeyeff?) and a secret examination begun. The answers were dictated by Tufeyeff; he surpassed himself on this occasion.

In order to nip the business in the bud, and to screen himself from the danger of making a second time an involuntary journey to Siberia, Tufeyeff instigated Mademoiselle Petroffsky to say, that she had been at variance with her brother since the Emperor Alexander passed through Perm, when she, being young and inexperienced, had been seduced by him, on which account she afterwards received 5000 roubles through General Solomka.

The habits of the Emperor Alexander were certainly of such a nature, as to make this story highly probable; it would have been difficult to ascertain the truth, at least, it would have given rise to a great deal of scandal.

To Count Benkendoff's enquiries, General Solomka answered: that so much money had passed through his hands, that he could not recollect those 5000 roubles.

"La regina en aveva molto", says the improvisatore in Pushkin's "Egyptian Nights".

And this honourable scholar of Araktjiyef, this noble comrade of Kleinmichel, this acrobat, vagabond, clerk, and governor, this delicate-minded, and disinterested man, who sent healthy people to the mad-house, and assassinated them, who calumniated the Emperor Alexander to escape the wrath of Nicholas, this same man now undertook to teach me my duties.

My state of dependence on him was very great. He need only write a word concerning me to the minister, and I should be sent to Irkutsk. It was not even necessary to write; he had the power to send any one where he liked, to some wild country like Kai or Zarevo-Santschursk, without mentioning it, without seeking for a pretext. Once he sent a young Pole to Glasoff, merely because the ladies rather preferred dancing the mazurka with him than with his Excellency.

In the same way, Prince Dolgorukoff was sent from Perm to Werchoturye. This place, hidden amongst mountains and snow, is still considered as belonging to the province of Perm, but resembles Berosoff in climate, and is worse than Berosoff, because it is a still larger desert. In winter time, the post only arrives once a month.

Prince Dolgorukoff belonged to these aristocratic idlers in the bad sense, who are but seldom found now-a-days. He had committed all sorts of tricks in Petersburg, Moscow, and Paris. He had spent his life like a second Ismailoff, on a smaller scale; as a Prince E. Grusinsky, without his asylum for deserters in Lyskowo. With all that, he was a spoiled, impertinent, disgusting charlatan, who played simultaneously the lord and the slave. At last, when his exploits passed all bounds, he was ordered to live in Perm.

He arrived there with two carriages; in the one he was seated himself, with his dog, in the second was his cook, a Frenchman, with his parrots. The arrival of the rich man occasioned great joy at Perm, and soon the whole town was assembled in his dining-room. He began an intrigue with a lady of Perm. This latter, suspecting the Prince not to be over faithful, went one morning unexpectedly to see him, and found him with his maid servant. This occasioned a scene which ended thus: The faithless lover took a whip from the wall; the lady guessed his intention, and ran away. He negligently dressed, in a mere *robe de chambre*, followed her to a place where the soldiers usually go to their manoeuvres, and gave the jealous lady some lashes. Then he returned home quietly, as though he had done something particularly meritorious.

By similar freaks, he roused the anger of Perm society, and the magistrates resolved on removing this mad-cap of forty, and sending him to Werchoturye.

The day before his departure, he gave a splendid dinner to the officers, and, notwithstanding their anger against him, they all appeared. Dolgorukoff had promised to regale them with a pastry of new and unheard of excellency. The pastry was in fact excellent, and disappeared with incredible rapidity. When nothing was left but the outer crust, Dolgorukoff turned to his guests and said, pathetically, "it shall not be said that I spared anything on my separation from you. Yesterday I had my 'Hardi' killed on purpose to make this pastry for you." The officers looked at each other with horror, and searched with their eyes for the well-known Danish dog. He was not to be seen! The Prince guessed their thoughts, and ordered the servant to bring the remains of Hardi, his skin and entrails. The rest was in the stomachs of the Perm people. Half the town fell sick with disgust.

In the meantime, Dolgorukoff departed triumphantly for Werchoturie, and was glad to have played so good a trick on his acquaintances. This time, a third carriage conveyed a whole hen-house. His fowls travelled with post-horses. On the way, he purloined the account books from several stations, changed them, altered the numbers, and drove the administrators of the post nearly mad, as, even with their books, they could hardly keep their accounts in order. The deadly emptiness and suffocating *ennui* of Russian life, and the lively and passionate characters, coupled with it *en mésalliance*, develop amongst us all sorts of monstrosities.

In the scornful laughter of Sonaroff, as in the dog-pastry of Prince Dolgorukoff, the wild rage of Ismailoff, and in the half good-humoured nonsense of Mamonoff, as well as in the bold crimes of Tolstoi, 'the American,' everywhere I hear the familiar sound which is known to us all, but which is controlled in many of us by cultivation of the mind, or the concentration of thought of some given subject.

I was particularly acquainted with Tolstoi, and principally at that epoch when he lost his daughter Sara, a remarkably gifted girl. A glance at that old man, at his forehead covered with grey hairs, his sparkling eyes, his athletic stature, showed how much nature had gifted him with strength and energy, but he had only developed in himself the stormy passions, the bad inclinations — and that is not to be wondered at — every vice is for a long while tolerated in Russia; but at the very first deed of a noble human passion, we are sent either to a garrison, or to Siberia.

For nearly twenty years Tolstoi had carried on; had fought duels, had maimed people, ruined whole families, until at last he was sent to Siberia. Thence he returned as 'an Aleutian', as Griboyedoff said, that is to say, he escaped through Kamtschatka to America, and there obtained permission to return to Russia.

The Emperor Alexander pardoned him, but immediately after his return, Tolstoi resumed his former life. He was married to a gipsy, known for her fine voice, and belonging to a band in Moscow. His house was converted into a gambling hell; days and nights were passed in drinking and playing at cards; and dreadful scenes of drunkenness and covetousness took place beside the cradle of little Sara. People say that he once put his wife on the table and shot the heel of her shoe off, to show the certainty of his aim.

His last trick was very nearly sending him a second time to Siberia.

He had long been angry with a certain citizen, and catching him one day, Heaven knows how, in his house, bound him hand and foot, and drew out one of his teeth. Does it seem credible that this could have happened only ten or twelve years ago?

The citizen, of course, made a complaint; Tolstoi bribed the police, as well as the Court of Justice, and the citizen was imprisoned as a liar. At the time, a very well known Russian author was on the commission of that prison. The citizen told him the circumstance, and the inexperienced officer resolved on taking the matter up.

Tolstoi was seriously frightened; for the affair appeared evidently to his disadvantage; but the Russian God is all-powerful. Count Orloff made a secret communication to Prince Schterbatoff, and advised him to let the affair drop, because it would not be well to give the lower classes any public triumph over the aristocracy. Count Orloff thought it moreover good to remove the literary official from such a position. This seems still more improbable than the story of the tooth extracting. I was at that time in Moscow, and knew the imprudent officer very well.

But let us return to Wiatka.

The office was, without comparison, much worse than the prison. The labour there was not too great; but what made it intolerable was the air of the infected spot suffocating as a kennel, and the absurd way of wasting time. Alenizia did not oppress me; he was even more civil than I expected. He had studied in a gymnasium in Kasan, and this made him respect a student of the Moscow University.

There were about twenty clerks in the office, for the most part people without the least instruction, and without a trace of morality. Children of clerks and secretaries, they were accustomed from the cradle to think and look at service as a profitable means of getting money, and to consider the peasants like a mine from which they have to extract gold. They were to be bribed with twenty and twenty-five kopecks, sold documents for a glass of wine, altered others, and degraded themselves in every possible way — in short, committed every meanness. My valet-de-chambre ceased to play at billiards, for he said the officers cheated more than anybody else, and he could not even chastise them for it, because they had the military rank. With these kind of people, then, whom my servant was prevented from striking, merely on account of their rank, I was obliged to spend every day, from nine to two in the morning, and from five to eight in the evening.

Besides Alenizia, who was chief of the entire office, there was a special head of each desk. My superior was not a bad man, but a drunkard who could scarcely read and write. At the same table with me, there sat four more clerks. I was forced to speak to and be acquainted with them, and, indeed, with all the others, not only because they would have taken my reserve for pride, and have played me some trick for it sooner or later, but because it would really have been impossible to spend daily several hours with the same people without becoming acquainted with them. Moreover, it must be remembered how people in provincial towns cling to newcomers, especially those who come from the capital, and more so when they happen to be the heroes of some interesting adventure.

Sometimes, when I had passed the whole day in this hell, I returned home in a sort of intellectual stupor, threw myself on the sofa, and felt miserable, enervated, degraded, incapable of any kind of work or occupation.

I regretted then, from my heart, my little cell in prison, with all its damp, its wood-lice, its gendarmes at the locked door — there I was free, did whatever I liked, was hindered by nobody, instead of these dull conversations, these dirty people, with their low ideas and coarse feelings — a death-like tranquillity, an uninterrupted peace prevailed there.

And when I recollected that I had to go again after dinner, and tomorrow again, and so daily, I was sometimes seized with a fit of rage and despair, and drank wine and brandy to console myself.

An additional annoyance was, that, at times, one or other of these companions in service looked in, *en passant*, just to kill the time, till the hour appointed for our re-appearance in the office.

Some months afterwards, however, the office became a little more supportable.

It is not in the Russian character to continue for any length of time the oppression of an individual, if there are no personal feelings, or no money interests in the case. This does not arise from any reluctance on the part of government to torment and ruin people; but it comes from Russian negligence, and from our *laisser aller*. The Russian magistrates are, in general, unpolished, presuming, bold; people are always exposed to their impertinence; but it is not in their nature to persecute a man incessantly. They give it up for want of patience; perhaps, also, because they gain no money by it. At first starting, they make a fuss which leads to nothing, partly to show their power, partly their zeal; but by and bye they leave you in peace.

So it happened in our office. The Ministry of Home Affairs had at that time a fit of love for statistics. It ordered committees to be chosen everywhere for that purpose, and sent round programmes of such a nature, as would scarcely have been executable in Belgium or Switzerland. It demanded at the same time all sorts of indices, with maximum and minimum, with averages and details of sums which had remained uncollected for more than ten years, and were not to be called in before the lapse of another year, t least. They even insisted on observations about the meteorological and moral state of the country.

The committee and those who gathered these particulars, received not a farthing; all this was to be done out of love for statistics. That love was supported by the police in the Governor's office. This office, overladen with work, and the Provincial Court of Justice, which hated all peaceful, theoretical occupations, looked upon the Statistical Committee as a useless article of luxury, a ministerial joke; nevertheless, it could not be helped: the accounts, with the indices and details, had to be made out.

The labour seemed inexpressibly difficult to all — nearly impossible; but that was their last care. They thought only how they could avoid being reprimanded. I promised Alenizia to draw up the introduction for the index, with some rhetorical sentences, foreign words, quotations, and remarkable details, on condition that he would allow me, in recompense for this great labour, to work at home, instead of in the office. Alenizia talked with Tufeyeff about it, and consented.

In my introduction to the report on the labours of the committee, I brought the hopes and expectations of that institution prominently forward, because, until now, it had effected nothing. Alenizia was deeply impressed by the production. Tufeyeff, himself, found it excellently written; with this ended my statistical labours, but the committee was put under my management. Henceforth, I was no longer forced to perform the horrible task of copying papers, and my drunkard of a president almost became my subordinate. Alenizia asked but for one thing: that for appearance's sake, I should go the office for a short time every day.

To prove how impossible it was to draw up really, systematic, and ably, I will introduce here a specimen of a report, which was sent to me from Kaï. Amongst various nonsense, it was said therein: "Drowned persons, 2; causes of drowning unknown; 2; total, 4."

Amongst the list of remarkable events, stood the following tragical anecdote:

"Citizen N, whose brain had been destroyed by the use of spirits, has hanged himself."

In another report, about the mortality of the inhabitants, it was said: "In the town of Kaï there are no Jews."

The only unhappy consequence of that same statistical labour, which saved me from office work, was a personal intercourse with Tufeyeff.

There was a time when I hated this man; that time is long past; the man himself is no more; he died about 1845, while residing at his estate near Kasan. Now I remember him without anger, like a curious animal, which I had met in a desolate forest, worthy of being studied; but which, from it being only an animal, could not possibly make me angry. At that time, it was not possible for me to avoid quarrelling with him; it would have been impossible for any honest man. Chance favoured me, else he would have certainly done me some injury, to punish my opposition; but, to be angry with him now for the evil he did not commit to me, would be ridiculous and lamentable.

Tufeyeff lived alone; he was divorced from his wife; the back part of the governor's palace was inhabited by his favourite, who, as if purposely, did not much study concealment. She was the wife of his cook, who was sent to a lonely village as a punishment for the crime of having married. This woman was not officially acknowledged, but those officers who were particularly attached to the governor, that is to say, who particularly feared enquiries, formed the court of the cook's wife. The wives and daughters of these officials paid her visits secretly in the evening, without boasting about them. This woman possessed the same tact by which Potemkin, one of her most famous male predecessors, had been distinguished. She herself chose such rivals for her lovers as could not be dangerous to herself; for she feared she might lose her situation, and knew, at the same time, the nature of her patron. Grateful for this disinterested attachment, he rewarded her by his devotion, and they lived in perfect harmony.

Tufeyeff was occupied the whole forenoon in the governmental office. At three o'clock the poesy of his life began. Dinner was no trifling matter for him; he was fond of eating, and principally of eating in society. In his kitchens, dinner was always prepared for twenty persons. If there were less than half that number he was displeased; if there were but two he was unhappy; if nobody came, he was nearly in despair, and went down in the apartments of his *chère amie*. It would not have been very difficult to find people who would have made it their daily habit to be fed there, but his official position, and the fear with which he inspired the officers, neither allowed them to profit by his hospitality, nor him to make a "restaurant" of his house.

He was therefore obliged to limit himself to state counsellors and presidents — with many of them he, however, disagreed; that is to say, they were in disgrace with him — celebrated travellers, rich merchants, farmers of the distilleries, and remarkable persons — something after the fashion of the *capacités* when, in the time of Louis Philippe, attempts were made to introduce into the elections. My readers will understand that I was a curiosity of the first rank in Waitka.

In the provincial towns people rather fear those who are sent there "on account of their opinions", but they are by no means taken for common mortals. "Dangerous people" possess, for provincials, the same charms which women find in celebrated Lovelaces, and men in courtesans. "Dangerous people" are much more avoided by the Petersburg officers and the Moscow magnates than by the inhabitants of the provinces, especially those of Siberia. Those who were exiled for the affair of the 14th December, enjoyed the highest esteem.

Munnich, in the Tower of Pelim, governed the whole province of Tobolsk. The governors went to him to consult him about important affairs. The lower classes are still less against the exiles; they are generally on the side of the punished. On the borders of Siberia, the name of "exile" disappears, and that of "unfortunate" is substituted. In the eyes of the Russian people, a man is not dishonoured when the Court of Justice has condemned him. In the province of Perm, in the streets of Tobolsk, the peasants are often seen to put milk, bread, and kwas — a sort of beer — on the sills of their open windows, to assist one of the "unfortunates", should he be escaping from Siberia.

A propos of the exiles! In Nyjnei we find exiled Poles; in Kasan, the number increases considerably. In Perm there were at that time forty; in Wiatka not less; besides which, in every small district town there are several.

They live quite separate from the Russians, and shun every intercourse with the inhabitants. The greatest union prevails among them, but no Russian is admitted into their society.

On the part of the inhabitants, I saw neither hatred, nor particular inclination towards them. They looked upon them as strangers; and the more so as not one of the Poles understood the Russian language.

An old and thoroughbred Sarmatian, who had been an officer in the time of Poniatowsky, and had shared a part of Napoleon's campaigns, received, in the year 1837, the permission to return to his possessions in Lithuania. The day before his departure, the old man invited me and some Poles to dinner. After dinner, when my host was a little elevated, he approached me with a drinking-cup, embraced me tenderly with soldier-like cordiality, and whispered in my ear: "Why are you a Russian?" I made no reply; but this observation fell heavily on my heart. I understood that this generation of Poles will not liberate Poland.

Since the time of Konarsky, however, the Poles look differently upon the Russians.

The exiled Poles have never been ill-treated; but the position of those who have no means is dreadful. From Government they receive but fifteen roubles banco a month, and with this money they must provide lodgings, board, fire, and clothing. In the larger towns, such as Kasan and Tobolsk, they can live by giving lessons and concerts, establishing drawing-classes, and playing at balls. But in Perm and Wiatka even these resources are wanting. Notwithstanding, they never ask the Russians for anything.

The invitations to Tufeyeffs luxurious sybaritic banquets were a real punishment for me. His dining-room was exactly like the office, only in another form; less dirty, but still more loathsome; for, apparently, people went there by their own free will, and not by compulsion.

Tufeyeff knew his guests perfectly; he despised them — showed them his fangs from time to time — sometimes shook his fist at them — and treated them, in general, as a master treats his dogs — sometimes with too much familiarity, and at another with so much rudeness, that it surpassed every limit. Yet he continually invited them to dinner, and they came, half by fear and half willingly — humiliated themselves, gossiped, spied, flattered, smiled, and bowed. I often blushed for them.

My friendship with Tufeyeff was of no long duration. He soon guessed that I was not fit for the "highest society" of Wiatka. After some months, he became discontented with me; a few more months passed, and he hated me. I not only did not partake of his dinners, but I never entered his saloons. A journey of the hereditary Prince of Russia through Wiatka, saved me from his persecutions, as we shall see presently.

I must observe, that I had done nothing in the world to attract, first, his attention and invitations, and afterwards, his anger. He could not bear to see in me a man who behaved independently, though in no way impertinently. I observed always a proper demeanour towards him; but that was not sufficient for him; he wanted to be flattered.

He loved his power jealously; had acquired it by the sweat of his brow, and he demanded not only obedience, but also the appearance of unlimited submission.

Unfortunately, in this he was national.

A landed proprietor is accustomed to say to his servant: "Be silent, I will allow no answer."

The chief of any department grows pale, and replies to his inferior, who ventures to make any opposition: "You forget yourself; do you know to whom you speak?"

The Emperor sends people in Siberia on account of mere opinions; torments people to death in the casemates on account of a few verses.

And all three of them are more willing to pardon theft, bribery, robbery, and murder, than the boldness of human dignity, and the audaciousness of free speech.

Tufeyeff was a true imperial servant; he was esteemed as such, but not sufficiently. Byzantine servitude, and official authority were in a rare harmony with him. The annihilation of his own self, the renunciation of self-will and self-thought before the supreme power, went perfectly together with the harsh yoke in which he placed his inferiors. He was well adapted to become a second Kleinmichel, and could have said like him: "Zeal overcomes all difficulties." Like the latter, he could have built the walls of the Winter Palace at the expense of men's lives, and have dried the building with men's lungs. He could equally well — or perhaps better — have beaten the young people from the engineers' department, because they would not become informers.

As a consequence of bitter experience, Tufeyeff nourished in his mind a deeply rooted, fiery hatred against everything that was aristocratic. Araktjiyeffs Chancelleries, a true hulk, was to him the first haven of liberation. Till then, his superiors had never offered him a seat; they had used him only for unimportant affairs. When he served in the military intendency, the officers persecuted him in a military way, and a colonel at Wilna had once beaten him with his whip in the open street. All this had sunk deep into the heart of the clerk, and the fruit had ripened. Now, as governor, it was his turn to oppress, not to offer a chair, to address people with insolence, to speak lower than necessary, and to summon even aristocrats of old families before his tribunal.

From Perm he had been removed to Twer. The aristocracy could not bear him notwithstanding his willingness to yield, and his slavish mind. The minister Bludoff displaced him once more at the request of the aristocracy, and sent him to Wiatka.

Here he again felt in his sphere. Here were officials, farmers of spirit distilleries, owners of mines, and manufacturers in any number he liked. All of them trembled and stood up before him; all of them feasted him and endeavoured to guess his wishes before they were uttered. At weddings and other festivals, the first toast was always to the health of his "excellency".

CHAPTER VIII

The Civil Officials — The Governor-Generals in Siberia —
A Rapacious chief of Police — A Tame Judge — A Roasted
Commissioner — A Tatar Apostle — A Boy of the Feminine
Gender — The Potato Revolution

One of the most lamentable results of the revolutions effected by Peter I, is the development of the caste of civil officials. This unnatural, uncultivated, hungry race of men understands nothing but "to serve", knows nothing except the rules and the forms of office. They represent a sort of secular hierarchy, who offer their worship, and build their altars in the courts of justice, and in the police offices, and whose eager impure lips suck the blood of the people.

Gogol[5] has unveiled some phases of their existence, and has shown us their loathsomeness in full relief. But he mollifies us involuntarily by his humour, and his hatred is foiled by his great comic talent. Besides, it was hardly possible for him, under the surveillance of the Russian censorship, to disclose the sad characteristics of this filthy lower world, in which the fate of the poor Russian people was moulded.

There, in these smoky offices, which we will hasten to quit, ragged people sit and write at first on grey paper, then on stamped paper, and according to the tenor of these papers, individuals, families, and whole villages are ill-treated, terrified, ruined. Fathers are sent to Siberia, mothers imprisoned, sons made soldiers; and all this comes upon them like a thunderstorm, unexpectedly, and, for the most part, quite undeservedly. And wherefore is all this? For money's sake. Be quick! make a collection, else you will be summoned under one pretence or another; for instance, an inquest will be held on the dead body of some drunkard, who has been burnt to death by ardent spirits, or frozen by the cold. To avoid this, the chief of the village (the starost) prefer making a collection, and the peasants bring their last farthing. The commissary of police

---

[5] A celebrated Russian writer, author of the "Dead Souls".

must live, and his wife also. The captain of the district must live and educate his children. Oh! he is a model of a father! This caste of civil officials is particularly numerous in the north-west provinces of Russia, and in Siberia. In these very distant provinces, it has been able to develop itself without impediment. There, all its members are occupied with their own gains alone; theft has become a *res publica*. Even the Imperial power, which generally fires grape-shot, is unable to pierce through this muddy, snow-covered cess-pool, full of thick dirt. All the measures which government has taken have been weakened; all their intentions misinterpreted. Government is continually cheated, made a fool of, or deluded; and all this is achieved amid the most devout, slavish subordination, and with the observance of the most minute official forms.

Speransky attempted to ameliorate the fate of the Siberian people. He introduced everywhere an administration of colleges, as if it were not all the same by whom theft was committed; by individuals or by members. He dismissed the old ruffians by hundreds, and introduced new ones by hundreds also. At first, he inspired the provincial police with such fears, that the officials themselves paid money to the peasants, in order to prevent them addressing petitions to the Governor. But a few years later, they had organised their robbery under a new form, which answered equally well with the old one.

Speransky was followed by another rarity, General Welyaminoff. During two years, he endeavoured to suppress the abuses prevalent in Tobolsk; but, seeing that his labours were without result, he left it off, and let affairs go on as they liked.

Others, who were cleverer than he, made no attempt at all; but filled their pockets, and left others to do the same.

"I will extirpate these briberies at their very root", said Senevin, the Governor of Moscow, to an old grey-haired peasant, who made a complaint about an undeniable wrong that had been done to him.

The old man smiled.

"Why do you laugh?" said Senevin.

"Ah, father!"[6] answered the peasant. "Pardon me; but I just recollected how, on one occasion, one of our brave ones boasted of his strength, and pretended to be able to lift the Great Tsar's canon at Moscow. He made the trial in reality; but he could not perform the feat."

Senevin, who related this anecdote himself, belonged to the small number of honest, but unpractical men in the Russian service, who believe that with a few rhetorical sentences, and with the extinction of two or three ruffians, the general epidemic of bribery can be cured. There are but two methods against it — publicity and an entirely different organization of the whole machine: as, for instance, the re-establishment of the old national way of judging by umpires, a jury, and *procès verbal*, and, in short, all that which the Government of St. Petersburg so bitterly hates.

Pestel, the Chief Governor of West Siberia (father of the famous Pestel, who was condemned to death by Nicholas) was like one of the most cruel pro-consuls of ancient Rome. He introduced a systematized public plunder into the whole country, which he closed against the other parts of Russia by his spies. No letter passed the frontiers without having been opened; and woe to the person who dared to blame his administration. Merchants of the first rank were imprisoned and put in chains for many years. He ordered them even to be tortured. Officers were sent to the frontiers of Eastern Siberia, and left there for years.

The people endured it for a long while. At last they resolved to bring the state of affairs to the ears of the Emperor, by means of a citizen of Tobolsk. The latter feared to do it in the usual way; he went, therefore, first to Ketcha, towards the east; there passed the Siberian frontier with a tea caravan. He found the opportunity of delivering his petition to the Emperor Alexander, in Zarskoe Selo, and entreated him to read it through. Alexander was astonished and surprised at the terrible account he read. He sent for the citizen, spoke a long while with him, and convinced himself of the real truth of the accusation. At

---

[6] The Russian peasants often address superiors with the name of Father.

last, he said to him, half sadly, half embarrassed: "Go now home, brother; the affair shall be examined."

"Your Majesty", said the citizen, "I cannot go home again. Rather order me to go to prison. My conversation with your Majesty will not remain a secret. I shall be killed."

Alexander started, and said to Miloradowitsch, who just then happened to be Governor-General of St. Petersburg: "You shall answer for his life."

"Then, allow me, your Majesty", said Miloradowitsch, "to take him with me to my own house." And so it happened. The citizen remained there until the affair was terminated.

Pestel nearly always resided in St. Petersburg; in this, resembling the pro-consuls, who were generally living at Rome. By his presence and his acquaintances there — but principally by his sharing his booty with others — he prevented all disagreeable rumours and accusations.[7]

The council of the Empire took advantage of Alexander's journey to Verona, or Aix-la-Chapelle, and resolved, for prudence and justice sake, to surrender the examination of the Siberian affairs to Pestel; the more so, as it just happened that Pestel was present in St. Petersburg, and as, of course, no one could be better able to judge of Siberian affairs. Miloradowitsch, Mordwinoff, and two other persons opposed this, however. The resolution and the affair were brought before the Senate.

The Senate helped Pestel out of every difficulty, by means of that same revolting influence, by which all the higher officials are supported; but Treskin, the Civil Governor of Tobolsk, was bereft of his titles and nobility, and sent to some place of banishment. Pestel was obliged merely to quit the service.

When Pestel's son was condemned to death, the father came in order to take leave of him. It is said that he addressed the son

---

[7] Count Rostopchin once took an opportunity for making a sharp allusion to Peter's conduct. After dining with the Emperor, they all three stood at the window, when the Emperor asked: "What can that black spot be on the cross upon the church?" "I am too short-sighted to distinguish it", answered Rostopchin; "your Majesty must ask Pestel; he has excellent eyes; he can see from here what happens in Siberia."

with terrible reproaches in the presence of spies and gendarmes, to show his own devotedness to the Emperor. He concluded this fatherly speech with the question, "And what was left thee to wish for?"

"That is too long to relate", answered the deeply offended son, "but amongst other views, I had also intended to render it impossible for governors like you to exist in future."

Pestel was followed in Siberia by Kapzewitsch, a pupil of the Araktjiyeff class. He was a thin, bilious tyrant; tyrant by nature, and by the customs of military service in which he had been brought up, a cruel officer. He himself determined the "maxima" of the prices of bribery; but the common business he left entirely in the hands of robbers.

In the year 1824, the Emperor intended to visit Tobolsk. Through the province of Perm, a broad, fine road, which has long been in use, and very likely is so good on account of the nature of the ground itself. Kapzewitsch, in order to receive the Emperor, had, in the lapse of a few months, a similar one made, leading to Tobolsk. In the spring, during a great frost, and at the first thawing of the snow, thousands of workmen were forced to work at the road, They were summoned for this work from the nearer and the more distant settlements. Sickness seized them, and one half of the workmen died. But zeal overcame all difficulties — the road was finished.

The east of Siberia is governed with still greater negligence. The distance is so great that news from there scarcely reaches St. Petersburg. At Irkutsk, was a governor who found a pleasure in firing off cannons in the middle of the town, when he was taking a walk, in a state of intoxication. Another, when he was quite drunk, used to dress in a full priest's dress, and performed divine service in the presence of the bishop. But at least the noise of the one and the devotion of the other, were not so injurious as Pestel's system of tyranny and Kapzewitch's uninterrupted cruel activity.

It is a pity that Siberia is so badly superintended. The choice of governors has always been of the worst kind. I don't know how Muravief, the present governor, behaves. He is renowned for his understanding and his abilities; but the others were good for nothing. Siberia has a great future; as yet, it is only looked upon as a reservoir which contains much money, furs, and other products of nature; but which is cold, covered with snow, poor in provisions and means of communication, and thinly peopled. All that, however, is not correct.

The Russian government, which kills everything, which produces nothing but by force, and by the stick, does not understand how to give that impulse of life, which would bring Siberia forward with American rapidity. We shall see what astonishing results will happen, when one day the mouth of the Amoor is opened for navigation, and when America meets Siberia on the confines of China.

I said long ago that the Pacific Ocean will be the Mediterranean of the future. In this future, the part of Siberia is most important, in consequence of its position between the Pacific, Southern Asia, and Russia. It is understood, of course, that Siberia must extend to the Chinese frontier. Why should we be obliged to tremble with cold in Beresof and Irkutsk, when there is a Krasnoyarsk?[8]

Even in the national character of the Russian population in Siberia, something exists which announces the possibility of another development. The Siberian race is well formed, healthy, clever, and prudent. The children of settlers, the Siberians, know nothing of the authority of the landed proprietors. There exists no nobility, and, consequently, no aristocracy in the towns. The officials and military officers, the representatives of the power, are rather like a hostile garrison, placed there by the conquerors, than like an aristocracy. The immense distances release the peasants from a too frequent intercourse with them. Money saves the merchants, who despise the officials in Siberia, and yield only apparently to them; but look on them as on what they really are, that is to say, their clerks of affairs in civil matters of business.

---

[8] A town which has a beautiful southern climate.

The use of arms, which is everywhere necessary in Siberia, with the habit of encountering danger, has rendered the Siberian peasant much more martial, dexterous, and more able to offer resistance than the Russian. The long distances which generally separate him from churches, have left his mind freer from superstition than is the case with the Russian. He is indifferent as to religion; there are a great many sectarians. In many of the more distant villages, the "Pope"[9] comes very rarely during the year; then he baptizes, marries and buries people, hears their confession, &c. for all the past time.

On this side of the Ural Mountains, the administration is somewhat better, and yet I could supply whole volumes of anecdotes about the abuses and frauds of the officials of all ranks, which I have seen and heard, during my service in the office and in the dining-room of the governor.

The Chief of Police of Wiatka once, in a confidential conversation, told me the following anecdote:

"My predecessor", he said, "was an extraordinary man; living in such a way, life has no difficulties; only one must be born for it. He was a kind of Seslavin or Figner"[10], and at these recollections, the eyes of the lame colonel — who had been raised to the dignity of a chief of police, on account of a wound he had received — sparkled with joy. "Not far from the town", he added; "a band of thieves had been noticed. The magistrates had been informed more than once, that money had been stolen from a brandy distillery, or merchandise had been taken away from a shop, &c. The governor was very angry, and wrote one order after the other. But, you know, the provincial police are very cowardly. If they are merely requested to catch one single little thief, they are willing enough to do so; but here it was the case of a whole band, who were, moreover, in all probability, armed

---

[9] A Russian priest.
[10] These persons were leaders of peasant bands, and carried on a Guerrilla war against the French in 1812 and 1813.

with guns; consequently, they did nothing. The Governor summoned the Chief of the Town Police,[11] and said to him:

'I know very well that this is not your business; but your ability induces me to apply to you.'

The Chief of the Police replied, 'that he had heard of the affair before' and added, 'In an hour, I will be on my way, your Excellency. I must take a party of soldiers with me. The thieves are at a certain place known to me; and in two or three days I will bring them to the provincial prison.'

So he did. With his party of soldiers, he surprised the thieves and brought them to town.

The trial began. The Chief of Police asked the thieves: 'Where is the stolen money?'

'We gave it to thee, father,' answered two of the thieves.

'To me!' said the Chief of Police, starting.

'To thee! To thee!' exclaimed the thieves.

'There's impudence for you', said the Chief of Police, growing pale with anger. 'You rascals; you had better say that I had helped you to rob. I will show you what it means to insult my uniform! I am a cavalry officer, and allow nobody to stain my honour.'

In consequence of this, they were beaten. They were to be made confess where the money was hidden. In the beginning, the thieves persisted in re-affirming what they had said; but when the Chief of Police ordered them to be beaten for two pipes, their leader exclaimed:

'We are guilty! The money has been spent in revelling.'

'Well! at last', said the Chief of Police. 'I am not to be so easily deceived, brothers.'

'No, very true. We ought to learn from your lordship, and not you from us. We are far behind you!' grumbled one of the old ruffians, looking with astonishment at the Chief of Police.

---

[11] The provincial police is elected by the peasants, the town police is appointed by the government.

The latter, however, got the Order of St. Wladimir at his button-hole, for this affair."

"'Will you allow me to ask you what the expression means 'for two pipes?' " said I, interrupting this long panegyric in favour of the chief of police.

"Well, that is a familiar expression among us. You understand that it is sometimes rather tiresome to witness the punishments, therefore we order the fellows to be beaten, and smoke a pipe the while; generally the execution is just over when a single pipe is smoked; but in extraordinary cases, you give the good fellows that pleasure during the time it takes you to smoke two pipes. The executioners are well practised, intelligent men; they know exactly how many strokes they have to give."

As a counterpart to this robber official, I will trace the portrait of another, the mild, tame, and despicable Tchinovnik.

Among my acquaintances was an old, honourable official, who had been dismissed from office in consequence of an inspection one of the senators had made in his province. He henceforth occupied himself with the composition of petitions, and the arrangement of private affairs within the magistrate's jurisdiction; the very things he was forbidden to do, when he was dismissed from office.

Fifty years ago, he had entered the service of the state; he stole, falsified documents, drew up false statements throughout three provinces, was three times accused before the court of justice, &c. This veteran of Russian police liked very much to tell striking anecdotes of himself and his companions in the state service, without ever concealing his contempt for the degenerated officials of the new generation.

"They are mere coxcombs", he used to say, "of course they also take their share of the plunder; it would be impossible to live without; but if you ask for dexterity or knowledge in the matter, you will not find it with them. I will give you an instance of one of my friends, who died last year. He had a head! He has left no bad memory in the minds of the peasants, although he has bequeathed a nice income to his family. This man had quite a peculiar way of managing things. When a peasant came to him with some affairs, he admitted him immediately, and was very kind and pleasant with him.

'What is thy name, my good fellow?' he would say, 'and what was thy father's name?'

The peasant bowed.

'My name is Yermolay, and my father was called Gregor.'

'Well, then, be welcome, Yermolay Gregoriewitch.[12] From what part of the country dost thou come by the help of God?'

'We are from Dubilowo.'

'I know; I know that place. The mills there at the right-hand side are probably yours?'

'Quite right; the mills belong to our community.'

'A rich village, excellent ground — garden ground?'

'Quite right, my Lord, we need not complain, thank God.'

'But it is necessary, my friend, that it be so. Thou, for instance, Yermolay Gregoriewitch, hast certainly to provide for a large family?'

'Three sons and two daughters; and then I took a boy into the house, besides, five years ago.'

'And perhaps thou hast also grandchildren?'

'Indeed, your Lordship, I have a few.'

'God be thanked! God be thanked! Increase and multiply! Well then, Yermolay Gregoriewitch, thou hast come a long way. Let us take a glass of birch-brandy.'

The peasant makes some excuses. The judge pours him out some brandy, and says:

'Hark ye, hark ye, my old fellow, the holy father of the church have not forbidden us to drink wine and oil on this day.'

'That's true: they have not forbidden it; but it is the same wine that brings men to mischief.' So saying, he makes the sign of the cross, bows, and drinks the brandy.

---

[12] In Russia, the sons are always called by the name of their fathers instead of a family name, adding the syllable "witch".

'It must be difficult to make end meet with such a family, Gregoriewitch. To nourish and clothe each of them well, one horse, and one cow cannot be sufficient. They would not give enough milk even.'

'For heaven's sake, patron, what could we do? with one horse only? We have three of them. I had also a fourth one — a dappled one, but it died on St. Paul's day of the evil eye. The carpenter in our village is, God preserve us, envious of another's prosperity.'

'Yes, yes, so it happens in this world. But your pastures must be very large. You doubtlessly have some sheep?'

'Of course, we have sheep.'

'Well, now I have chattered away my time, Yermolay Gregoriewitch. The service of the Tsar is very exacting, and I must hasten to the office. Hast thou any business with me?'

'Yes, your Lordship, I have.'

'Well, what is it? Hast thou quarrelled with anybody? Be quick, my friend, tell me in haste, it is time for me to go.'

'Aye, my good Lord, I have had bad luck in my old days. You see it was about the time of the Assumption, when we were in the public-house. Well, and then, we spoke somewhat strongly with a peasant from the neighbourhood, a rude fellow, who steals the wood from our forest.

When we had talked together, he raised his hand, and struck me on the chest with his fist.

Thou should'st not beat people in a strange village, I said, and meant — that is to say, merely as an example to give him a push; but God knows how it came; was it by drunkenness or the evil spirit, I hit him just in the eye. Well, and so I have somewhat spoiled his eye; he went immediately to the Chief of Police with the churchwarden, and he says he will bring the case before the Court of Justice.'

During this tale, the judge (what are your St. Petersburg actors in comparison with him?) grows more and more serious, looks terrible and says not a word.

The peasant observes it and turns pale; he puts his hat down at his feet, and draws forth from it a sort of towel, in order to dry the perspiration on his brow. The judge keeps silent and turns over the leaves of a book.

'This is the reason why I have come to thee, my patron', the peasant again begins, in a voice that is scarcely like his own.

'But what can I do in it? what an accident; and why then, hit him just in the eye?'

'Indeed, the evil spirit must have seduced me.'

'I am very sorry, very sorry; if we consider too, that a whole household will be ruined! How shall the family live without thee? a lot of young people, and the grandchildren, still more babies, and thy wife too, how I pity her!'

The legs of the peasant begin to tremble. 'How so, my patron? to what have I brought myself?'

'Look, Yermolay Gregoriewitch, read it thyself, or art thou not conversant with the art of reading? well, then, look, the article about maiming the limbs.

After the punishment of the knout, to be sent to Siberia.'

'Let not a man be ruined, hurl not a Christian into misery! Is there help in any way?'

'Thou art a curious fellow! how can one alter the law! Of course everything is but the work of man's hand! well, instead of the thirty blows, we will only administer about five.'

'Yes, but the other part, about Siberia?'

'That is not in our power, my friend.'

Now the peasant draws a purse from his pocket, takes a paper out of it, opens the paper, extracts two or three gold pieces from it, and, with a deep bow, puts them upon a table.

'What does this mean, Yermolay Gregoriewitch?'

'Save me, patron!'

'Stop, stop! What an idea! I, poor sinner, accept sometimes a token of gratitude; for my salary is but very moderate — I am forced to accept it; but if one does it, it must, at least, be for some purpose. How can I help thee? Had it been only a tooth, or a rib — but, just the eye! Take your money back!'

The peasant stands overwhelmed.

'Or, perhaps, I might be able to manage it in the following way: — I might talk about it with my colleagues, and write, also, to the capital of the province. It is possible that the affair will be brought before the Provincial Court of Justice, wherein I have friends; They will be willing to do everything; but they are people of quite a different kind. For them, one or three gold pieces are not sufficient.'

The peasant recovers somewhat.

'As to me, thou needest not give me anything. What I do, I do out of mere pity for the family; but the others would not look at it, if they were not offered, at least, two 'greys.[13]'

'For God's sake, I don't know from where I am to get such an immense sum of money? Four hundred roubles! — and the times are so bad!'

'Yes; I believe that it may be difficult. Well, we will soften the punishment, in regard, shall we say, of thy repentance, and of thy having done it in a state of intoxication. There is some humanity even in Siberia! — moreover, it is not so very far for thee to go there! Of course, a couple of horses, one of the cows, and the sheep sold — that would be sufficient. But, certainly, for a peasant, it is a hard thing to provide so much money. On the other hand, supposing that the horses will remain, thou wilt be obliged to go where *no shepherd ever drove his flock*! Think of that, Gregoriewitch; there is still time; we will wait till tomorrow. But now I must hurry away', added the judge, pocketing the gold pieces which he had at first refused, and saying: 'It is quite superfluous: but I merely take them not to offend you.'

But see! The following morning the old Jew of a peasant brings to the judge about three hundred roubles banco, collected in different kinds of doubloons and ancient roubles.

---

[13] The grey banknotes were worth 200 francs (£8) before 1839. The other mentioned gold pieces are of 20 shillings worth.

The judge promises his protection; the peasant is summoned before the court of justice.

They are long in judging him; for a long time he is intimidated and imprisoned; and at last he is dismissed with a slight punishment, or with the advice to be more cautious in future; or with the registry against him, of being left as suspected.

The peasant prays all his life long to God, for the welfare of his judges".

The old official used to add: "Thus things were done in former times. They were always entirely settled."

*****

The peasants of Wiatka are, for the most part, not very enduring; therefore, the officials call them calumniators and unquiet people. But a real gold-mine for the officials are the Watiakes, the Mordwines, the Tchuwashes, poor, miserable, timid people. The under officials pay a double tribute to the governors, when they send them to districts inhabited by Finns. With these wretched beings, the police and officials do incredible things.

If a surveyor passes, for any purpose, through a Watiakish village, he certainly stops there, fetches from his cart the astrolabium, drives a pale into the ground, and spreads the chain.

Scarcely an hour has elapsed, when the whole village is in alarm and consternation.

"The land measuring! the land measuring!" the peasants say, with the same expression of terror as people said, in 1812, "The French! the French!" Then comes the alderman, with the elders of the village, to pay his visit to the officer. This latter, however, continues to measure, and to write down notes. The alderman begs him not to diminish their land, not to injure them so much. The geometrician demands from twenty to thirty roubles. The Watiakes are thankful for this proposal, collect the money; and the surveyor continues his journey to the next village.

If the chief officer of a district, and the chief of police, find a dead human body, they carry it, for some weeks, all about the Watiake villages, thanks to the cold which renders this possible.

In every village, they say that they have just found the corpse, and that a trial will be held in that place.

Then the Watiakes prefer giving a ransom.

Some years before my arrival, it happened that a chief officer, who had made it his business to collect ransoms, brought a corpse into a large Russian village, and demanded about two hundred roubles. The alderman assembled the parish; they would not give more than one- hundred. The officer would not yield. The peasants then grew angry, shut him up, together with his two secretaries, in the Common Hall, and threatened to burn them therein. The officer would not believe in this menace. The peasants put straw around the house, and offered the officer, as an ultimatum, a bank note for one hundred roubles, at the point of a stick, through the window. The heroic officer asked one hundred more; and, thereupon, the peasants fired the house from all sides; and the three Mucü Seevolac of the provincial police were burnt. This matter was eventually brought before the Senate.

The Watiake villages arc, in general, much poorer than the Russian.

"You have a wretched habitation", I said to a Watiake innkeeper, in whose damp, smoky, half-ruined hut I was obliged to wait for post horses, whilst I put aside a glass of stinking milk, which he had presented to me.

"What is there to be done, my father? We poor people spare our money for the black day."

"Well, there can scarcely be any day blacker than this one, my old fellow", I replied, pouring him out, at the same time, a glass of rum. "There, drink a glass to console you!"

"We don't drink, my father", answered the Watiake, looking passionately at the glass, and mistrustfully at me.

"Don't be silly! Take it!"

"Drink first, then!"

I drank, and then the Watiake drank also.

"And who art thou?" he asked. "Thou come'st, perhaps, from the government, on some business?"

"No", said I. "I am only passing through. I am going to Wiatka."

This evidently tranquillised him; and after having looked all around, in order to assure himself that no one was listening, he added, as if for an explanation:

"Black day when chief officer and priest come."

About the latter, I have to make some observations.

The priest in Russia becomes more and more a spiritual police officer, as is to be expected from the Byzantine humility of our Greek Church, and from our imperial popery. One part of the race of the Finlanders had accepted baptism, even before the time of Peter I.; another part was baptized during the reign of the Empress Elizabeth; but a third is still heathen to this very day; and even those who were baptized, during the reign of Elizabeth, clung in secret to their old, gloomy, wild faith.[14] Every two or three years, the Chief Officer, or the Head of the Police, (Stanovoi) with the priest, passes through the villages in order to investigate who of the Watiakes has been to the Lord's Supper, and who has not, and why. They are then oppressed in every way; imprisoned, whipped, and they must pay. But the Chief of Police and the priest, try before everything else to collect proofs that these poor people have not given up their former religious ceremonies.

After some proof has been found, the spiritual spy and police missionary make a noise. They ask an immense ransom, make "black day", and drive off, leaving everything as it was, in order to have an opportunity some years later of coming again with rod and cross.

In the year 1835, the Holy Synod thought it necessary to apostolize a little in the district of Wiatka, and to convert the Tcheremisses (heathens) to the right faith. This conversion is a type of all the great ameliorations accomplished by the Russian gov-

---

[14] All their prayers are reduced to the one material request; viz., for the continuation of their race, for a good harvest, the preservation of the flocks, and nothing more. "Give, Jumala, that from one buck there come two; from one grain five; that my children may have children again." In this uncertainty about earthly life and daily bread there is something decrepid, oppressed, and sad. They esteem the devil (Schaitan) as highly as God.

ernment — empty show, decorations, lies, brilliant accounts, and — somebody flogged.

The metropolitan Philaretes sent a dexterous missionary. His name was Kurbanowsky.

Suffering from the Russian disease, ambition, he took up the conversion most zealously, and resolved to present the Tcheremisses with the grace of God, at any price.

Firstly he tried it on with sermons; but he was soon wearied of this expedient; nor, in fact, can much be done by these old, worn-out means at the present day.

Soon perceiving the meaning of this procedure, the Tcheremisses sent their own priests, wild, fanatic, and clever, men. After long discussions, they said to Kurbanowsky:

"In the forest there are white birch-trees, high firs and pines; and there are likewise small juniper bushes. God suffers them all, and does not order the bush to be a pine. We men are like those bushes in the forest. Be you the white birch trees, we will remain the juniper bushes. We do not hinder you; we *pray for the Tsar*, pay our taxes, and furnish recruits; but will not become faithless to our religion."

Kurbanowsky understood that he was not able to convince them, and that the character of a Cyrillus or a Methodius[15] would not be his. He consulted the chief official of the district.

This latter was exceedingly glad. For a long time he had wished to display his zeal for the church. He was an anabaptized Tatar, that is to say, an orthodox Mussulman, whose name was Dewle-Kildeyeff.

He took with him a detachment of soldiers, and went to bombard the Tcheremisses with the word of God. Several villages were baptized. The apostle Kurbanowsky sang a Te Deum for joy, and returned in all humility to his home, in order to receive his ordination. The Tatar apostle got the order of St. Wladimir from government, as a remuneration for the propagation of Christianity.

---

[15] The first who preached Christendom in Russia.

Unfortunately, the Tatar missionary was not on very good terms with the Mollah in Malmyjy. The latter was excessively displeased that an orthodox son of the Koran preached the Gospel so zealously. During the Ramazan, the Tatar official appeared in the mosque with his order hanging from his button-hole in a most swaggering way, and placed himself, as usual, in front of all the other people. The Mollah had just begun to read the Koran, with a nasal voice, when he suddenly stopped, and said he could not proceed in the presence of an orthodox person, who had come into the mosque, with the sign of the foe.

The Tatars began to murmur, the official grew confused, hid himself somewhere, and took off his order.

Some time later, I read in the monthly paper of the Ministry for Home Affairs, an account about this splendid conversion of the Tcheremisses. In this account, the zealous endeavours of Dewle-Kildeyeff were also mentioned. Unluckily, it was forgotten to add that his zeal for the church was the more disinterested, the more firmly he adhered to Islamism.

*****

Before the end of my sojourn in Wiatka, robbing had become a regular custom in the department of "Crown Estates" to such a degree, that a commission was named for sending commissaries all through the provinces, for the purpose of a general supervision. A new system of administration for the Crown peasants was the result of this measure.

The Governor, Korniloff, had also to name two commissaries. I was one of those two. What incredible things did I see there! Many sad, many ridiculous, many disgusting; but the most astounding were the titles of the trials. For instance, "A trial about the building for the Provincial Magistrate, which building has been lost without any person knowing where it was left, and about the plan of the same eaten up by mice."

"A process about two and twenty Crown farms, which have been lost."

"A trial about the peasant boy Wasily (William) being registered among the feminine sex."

This last title was so striking, that I read through the whole trial, from the beginning to end.

The father of this said Wasily writes in his petition to the Governor, that a daughter had been born to him fifteen years before, whom he intended to call Wasilisa (Wilhelmina); but the priest, who was drunk, baptized her as Wasily, and registered her as such. The father cared little for this circumstance at first; but when he thought it would soon be his turn to furnish a recruit, and to pay the poll-tax, he informed the Starost of the affair. The police considered this case to be exceedingly difficult. At first, they refused to admit the case at all, because the peasant had allowed the term of ten years to elapse. Thereupon, he went to the Governor. The latter ordered an official statement from a physician and a midwife to be laid before him, to see whether this boy really were of the female sex. Thereupon followed, Heaven knows why! a correspondence between the Consistory, and the priest (the successor to the drunkard, who, through a superfluity of modesty, had not been able to distinguish the sexes) took a part in the affair. It went on for years, and perhaps ended with a suspicion for ever resting on the girl, of being a boy.

My readers must not take this for a droll imagined tale on my part. On the contrary, it is entirely in the spirit of Russian aristocracy.

In the time of the Emperor Paul, a Colonel of the Guards had in his monthly report entered an officer, who had been taken to the hospital in a desperate condition, as being dead.

Paul ordered his name to be erased from the Army List. Unfortunately, the officer did not die, but recovered. The colonel persuaded him to retire for a few years to his estates, hoping to find means, in the meanwhile, to correct the error. The officer agreed to it; but, unluckily, his heirs had read the advertisement of his death, and would now, by no means, recognize him as still alive. Inconsolable on account of the death of their dear relative, they asked to be immediately acknowledged as proprietors of the inheritance. When the living deceased now perceived that a second death awaited him — not by command, but by starvation — he travelled to St. Petersburg, and presented a petition to Paul. Paul wrote upon it with his own hand, "A supreme order has already been issued about this affair; his request is refused."

This surpasses even the case of Wasily-Wasilisa. What is the common fact of life, in comparison with a supreme order? Paul was the poet and dialectician of Autocracy.

However muddy this pool must be, still I cannot refrain from stirring it up with a few more words. The publication of those sad circumstances is the only poor atonement for the sufferers, who have perished there, without any consolation, and any record of their fate.

The government likes to give uncultivated land, as remuneration to the higher officials. This is no great evil, although it would be more prudent to keep the land for the increasing population. The rules, according to which the land is allowed to be distributed, are pretty well fixed. The banks of such rivers as serve for navigation are not permitted to be given: nor both the banks of a river, at the same time; no wood serviceable for building; and, in no case, such land as is cultivated by peasants, even if the peasants have no other rights upon it than the right of superannuation.[16]

But all these rules are, of course, only valuable on paper. In fact, the measuring of the ground for private property, is an immense source of robbery for the government, and of oppression for the peasant. If a nobleman of old family gets such a property, he generally sells his rights upon it to merchants, or seeks, in spite of the laws, to appropriate to himself something extraordinarily good, by the help of the magistrates themselves.

---

[16] The peasants in the province of Wiatka have a particular predilection for removing. Very often, two or three new settlements are all at once seen in the woods. Immense pieces of land and large forests (already half-rooted out) seduce the peasants to take possession of these useless grounds. The ministry for Home Affairs has already several times been forced to secure the land as property to the settlers.

Even Count Orloff had received, as if by chance, the part of a road and of a pasture, where the cattle that comes from the province of Saratow is accustomed to stop.

Therefore, it is not to be wondered at, that, one fine morning, a peasant from the district of Darov saw his land cut off up to the very farm, and given, as private property, to a merchant who had bought land of one of Count Cancrin's relations. The merchant fixed an annual tax, as a rent for the land. Hence issued a law-suit. The Court of Exchequer, which had been bribed by the merchant, and feared Cancrin's relations, complicated the affair. But the peasants were resolved to carry on the cause in earnest. They elected two of their most able men, and sent them to St. Petersburg. The affair came before the Senate. The department for land-measuring guessed that the peasants were in the right; but did not know what to do, and, therefore, asked Cancrin. Cancrin confessed quite plainly that the land was not rightly taken, but that it would be very difficult to restore it, because it had, in the meanwhile, already been sold to somebody else, who had spent a great deal of money in improving the property. His excellency, who had a vast deal of government property under his superintendence, concluded that a sufficient compensation of land should be given to the peasants on the other side. All were pleased with this sentence, except the peasants. Firstly, it is no trifle to begin cultivating a field upon entirely virgin land; and, secondly, it was proved that the land on the other side was not so well situated, and was marshy. And, as the Darov peasants did not occupy themselves so much with shooting snipes, as with agriculture, they presented a second petition.

But the Court of Exchequer, and the Ministry of Home Affairs, made a new lawsuit of it; and, referring to a law which decreed that, in case uncultivable land should be found among the territory given to a parish, this could not be left out in the measuring, but that, in such a case, a part half as large as that already granted, should be added; they, likewise added half a swamp, to the whole one given before.

The peasants protested and applied to the Senate; but during the time in which their case was before the tribunal, they received from the department from the land measuring, the plan of their new possession, in a rich cover, as usual, painted and ornamented with the star of the winds, and interesting explanations about the rhombus, R. Q. Z., and the rhombus Z. Q. R. At the same time, they were required to pay the considerable costs for the measuring. The peasants, seeing that they should not only not have their land, but that they, moreover, should be obliged to pay, refused positively the payment.

The chief official of the district sent a report of this to Tufeyeff. This latter sent a detachment of soldiers there under the command of the Chief of Police of Wiatka. On their arrival, they seized several of the peasants, had them beaten with rods, appeased the district in this way, took money; surrendered the "guilty" persons to the court of justice, and were for several weeks afterwards quite hoarse from the continued shouting. Several people were sentenced to be flogged, and sent to Siberia.

Two years later, the hereditary Grand Duke travelled through the district of Darov. The peasants presented a petition. He ordered the prayer thereof to be examined into. I had to draw up the report. What has been the result of this revision I have never learned. I have only heard that the exiled were permitted to return; but I have not heard that their land has been restored.

In conclusion, I will mention the famous story of the potatoe revolution.

The Russian peasants did not like to plant potatoes, as formerly the peasants throughout Europe disliked it, just as if people had an instinctive knowledge that these vegetables formed a bad kind of nourishment, imparting neither strength nor health. On the property of many well-meaning landlords, however, and in several villages belonging to government, potatoes were planted long before the potatoe revolution took place. But the Russian government precisely dislikes all those things that are done in a natural and quiet way. They want them to be executed under the impulse of the stick, and the fugleman, and by military command.

In the Government of Kasan, and part of Wiatka, the peasants had planted their fields with potatoes. When these potatoes were gathered, the ministry formed the idea of establishing central pits in each district. The project for the pits is confirmed, the pits are ordered, the pits are prepared, and in the beginning of winter the peasants carry, with a heavy heart, the potatoes to the central pits.

But when, in the following spring, they were to be forced to plant the frozen potatoes, they refused to obey. And, in fact, a more revolting insult could not be inflicted on labour, than to command it to do something evidently absurd.

The refusal, however, was regarded as rebellion. The Minister Kisseleff sent an official from St. Petersburg. This latter, a clever and dexterous man, took in the first district he reached, one rouble from each individual, and then relieved them from planting the potatoes. He repeated this proceeding in a second and third district. In the fourth one, the chief of the parish told him very decidedly, that he would neither plant potatoes nor give him money.

"You have exempted such and such districts", he said to him, "consequently it is clear that you must likewise exempt us."

The official tried to terminate the affair by threats and blows, but the peasants seized sticks and pales, and forced the division of police to fly.

The military governor sent Cossacks. Thereupon the neighbouring districts took the part of their brothers. In short, guns and cannons had to be employed; the peasants left their houses, and went into the forest.

The Cossacks drove them out of the jungle like wild beasts; they were seized, put into chains, and sent to Kosmodemyansk, before a military commission.

The old colonel of the garrison happened, by chance, to be an honest, plain-minded man. He declared openly, that the only guilty party in the affair was the official sent from St. Petersburg. Then all the other members of the Commission fell upon him; his voice was drowned; he was frightened — yes! even ashamed, as they reproached him with the intention of ruining an innocent man.

The trial took its course, as is usual in Russia. The peasants were beaten at the examination — beaten as a punishment — beaten as an example — beaten for money; and a great many of them were sent to Siberia.

It is remarkable that Kisseleff passed through Kosmodemyansk whilst the examination was going on. I think it might have come into his mind to look into the Military Commission, or to call the Colonel, and talk with him. He did not do it! —

When the famous Turgot saw the dislike of the French for potatoes, he sent potatoe-seed to the government farmers, to the purveyors, and other people subordinate to him, forbidding them to give any to the peasants. At the same time, however, he let them know indirectly, that they need not prevent the peasants from stealing potatoe-seed. Some years later a great part of France was planted with potatoes.

After all, my Lord Kisseleff, is not that better than grape-shot?

CHAPTER IX

Alexander Witberg

Amidst these deformed, filthy, paltry, and disgusting persons, scenes, occupations, and titles, in this Chancery system, and this court of justice, there are traced in my memory the sorrowful and noble features of an artist ruined by government with cold, unfeeling cruelty.

The iron hand of the Tsar has not only nipped in the bud the artist's work, full of genius; has not only ruined his productive powers, by entangling him in a thousand meshes, of judicial and political proceeding — but has also tried to bereave him of his bread, and his honest name; representing him as a bribe-taker, and a stealer of public money.

When Nicholas had ruined the artist, he sent him to Wiatka. There I met him.

I lived with him two years and a half, and saw this strong man succumb to the burden of persecutions and misfortunes — a victim to that civil and barrack system of absolutism, that measures everything idiotically by a recruit's measuring-staff and Chancery office-compasses.

It cannot be said that he yielded easily. During full ten years he struggled desperately. He even brought to the place of exile, the hope of triumphing over his enemies, and of justifying himself; in short, he arrived there still prepared for the fight — filled with plans and hopes. But there he soon saw that all hope was at an end.

And, perhaps, he would even have overcome this; but he had a wife and children by his side, and before him years of exile, of misery, of privations — and Witberg grew grey and more grey, older and older, with every day — yes, with every hour!

When I left him, after two years' acquaintance in Wiatka, he had aged at least ten years.

The story of his long martyrdom is as follows:

The Emperor Alexander had no faith in his victory over Napoleon; that glory was a burden for him — he conferred it upon God. From his youth inclining to mysticism, and to gloomy thoughts (in which several persons thought they saw torments of conscience), he particularly gave way to this torn of thought, after having obtained a series of victories over Napoleon.

When "the last soldier of the enemy had stepped across the frontier", Alexander published a manifesto, in which he uttered a vow to build in Moscow a colossal church, in honour of the Saviour.

He asked for plans on all sides. A great competition was to take place.

Witberg was a very young artist at that time, who had just terminated his studies, and received a golden medal for some paintings of Swedish origin. He was born in Russia, and educated at first in the Corps of the Cadets for the Mines. The exalted, eccentric young artist, with his mystic views reads the manifesto — reads the summons — and abandons all his avocations. Days and nights he wanders about the streets of St. Petersburg, incessantly pursued by one sole idea. It overpowers him; he shuts himself up in his room, seizes the pencil, and begins his work.

The artist confided what he is meditating to no human being. After some months' work, he travels to Moscow, in order to study the city and environs; and then begins anew to work, hiding himself and his labour from the world's eyes.

The time of competition began. The plans were manifold. There were some sent from Italy, some from Germany; all our academicians had submitted theirs, and, among others, the young unknown artist. Weeks passed before the Emperor took notice of the plans. Those days were for Witberg the forty days in the desert — the days of temptation, of doubt, of tormenting expectation.

Witberg's colossal plan, filled with religious poetry, struck Alexander. He left off looking at the others, and asked by whom this plan had been presented. The packet was unsealed, and the unknown name of a scholar of the academy was found.

Alexander wished to see Witberg. He conferred a long time with the artist. His bold and fiery words, the true enthusiasm with which he was penetrated, and the mystic turn of his convictions, made a deep impression upon the Emperor. "You speak through stones", he observed, looking again at the plan.

The plan was accepted that very same day, and Witberg was named to build the church, and to be the director of the committee for the building. Alexander did not imagine that, together with the laurel wreath, he was putting upon the artist's brow the crown of thorns.

No art is more nearly related to mysticism than architecture. Abstract, geometrical, silently musical, passionless architecture lives by symbolism, by forms, by indications. Plain and simple lines, their harmonious proportions, their rhythm, their numbers, present something mysterious, and at the same time incomplete. Buildings, or temples, do not contain their object within themselves, like the statue, the picture, the poem, the symphony; the building waits for the inhabitant; it is a limited, untenanted space, a surrounding exterior, the coat of mail of a tortoise, the shell of a mollusc, and the task is, that the cover be so in accordance with the spirit of the object, or the inhabitant, as the coat of mail is in accordance with the tortoise. Upon the walls of a temple, in its arches and columns, its portal and façade, its basis and cupola, the deity that lives within must be impressed, as the folds of the brain are impressed upon the bones of the skull.

The temples of the Egyptians were their Holy Scripture, the obelisks were sermons in the high road. Solomon's temple is the bible in stone, and such is the church of St. Peter — a petrified offspring of Catholicism — the beginning of a worldly world — the beginning of the secularization of humanity.

From ancient times, the erection of temples has been full of mysteries, ceremonies, allegories, mysterious consecrations; so that, in the middle ages, the architects thought themselves a particularly consecrated people, a sort of ecclesiastics, descendants from the architects of Solomon's temple; and they founded among themselves the mysterious associations of stone-masons, which afterwards changed into free-masonry.

Architecture loses its peculiar mystic character in the time of the revival of art. The Christian Faith wrestles with philosophic scepticism, the Gothic arch with the Grecian cornice, spiritual holiness with worldly beauty. Hence the Church of St. Peter has such high importance. In its colossal dimensions, Christendom begins to breathe life; the church becomes Pagan, and Buonarotti paints Christ on the walls of the Sixtine Chapel, as a broad shouldered athlete, as a Hercules in the full bloom of his years and strength.

After the erection of the Church of St. Peter, the art of building churches completely declined, and was at last reduced to a simple repetition, in different sizes, partly of the antique Hellenic periptery, partly of the style of St. Peter. In Paris, a Parthenon was called the church of Ste. Magdalene; in New York, the Exchange.

Without belief, and without particular inspiring circumstances, it was difficult to produce anything new. Constraint, hypocrisy, anachronism, were visible in all the modern churches. As, for instance, in those "*plat menages*" with five towers, and onions instead of cork-stoppers, in the Indo-Byzantine style, which Nicholas erected by the assistance of M. Thow; or, in the tasteless Gothic churches with which the English adorn their cities, and which offend every artistic eye.

But the circumstances under which Witberg conceived his plan, his individuality, and the disposition of mind of the Emperor Alexander were very uncommon.

The war of 1812 had violently shaken the mind of Russia. Long after the deliverance of Moscow, the deeply agitated thoughts, and the excited nerves of the nation could not be so easily tranquillized. Events abroad, the entrance into Paris of the allied troops, the history of the Hundred Days, the expectations, the rumours, Waterloo, Napoleon exiled far across the ocean, the mourning for killed relations, the anxiety for the still living, home returning, warriors; all this together had a deep effect, even upon the rudest natures. Now imagine a youth, an artist, who has a disposition to mysticism, who is endowed with creative power, fanatic, impressed by the rapidly passing events, by the imperial summons, and under the influence of his own genius.

Not far from Moscow, between the roads of Mojaisk and Kaluga is an elevation which commands the whole town. It consists of those "sparrow mountains" which I have mentioned in the recollections of my youth. The whole city lies extended at their base. From their summit one of the most beautiful views of Moscow is enjoyed. There stood John the Terrible, then still a young, extravagant man, and looked weeping at his burning capital; here the priest Sylvester stepped before him, and changed the young paragon for the next twenty years by his severe admonition.

Round this mountain, Napoleon went with his army; here his forces were broken; from the foot of the Sparrow Mountains began the retreat.

Would it have been possible to find a more suitable place for the erection of a monument in remembrance of the year 1812, than the farthest spot reached by the enemy's advance.

But this was not enough. The mountain itself was to be converted into the lower part of the church; the plain, thence to the river, was to be surrounded by columns; and upon this basis, built by nature herself on three sides, a second and a third temple were to be erected, which altogether were to present one vast unity. Witberg's church is like the chief dogma of Christendom, triune and indivisible.

The lower temple cut out of the mountain bore the form of a parallelogram, of a coffin, of a corpse; its exterior represented a portal of great artistic value, supported by columns in the Egyptian style. The temple itself, ended in the interior of the mountain, losing itself in the unchiselled depth of mother earth. This temple was illuminated by lamps upon high Etruscan candelabra. Daylight entered scantily from the second temple, through a transparent picture, representing the birth of Christ. In this crypt, all the heroes fallen in the year 1812, were to repose; requiems were continually to be held for those killed on the battle field, and their names, from the general's to the soldier's, were to be cut into the stone of the walls.

Above this churchyard, this coffin, the equilateral Grecian cross of the second temple extended itself in all four directions; the temple of the arms outspread upon the cross, the temple of life, of suffering, and of trouble. The colonnade, which leads to it, was ornamented with statues of the personages of the Old Testament. At the entrance stood the prophets. They stood outside the temple, pointing the way to it, which they themselves were not allowed, however, to enter. In the interior of this temple, the whole story of the Gospel, and the deeds of the Apostles were represented.

Beyond this second temple, crowning and closing them all, was a third one, built in the form of a rotunda. This last, splendidly lighted, was the temple of the spirit, of un-disturbable quiet, of eternity, which was symbolised in the circular shape of the building. There were no images of saints, no pictures, only at the outside it was surrounded with a garland of archangels, and covered by a colossal cupola.

I have now tried to render, according to my recollections, Witberg's principal idea. It was worked out by him in the most minute details, and everywhere corresponded exactly with the Christian idea, and the rules of architectural beauty.

Extraordinary man as he was, he worked in execution of his design through his entire life. During the ten years he was under the persecution of justice, he occupied himself constantly with it. In exile, tormented by want and misery, he dedicated every day several hours to the accomplishment of his plan. This church was his life; he could not believe that it would not be built: his portfolio contained his recollections, his consolation, his fame, his everything.

Perhaps after the death of the martyr, a happier artist will shake the dust from these plans and publish with reverence this architectural martyrology, in which a vigorous life extinguished itself, and departed overpowered with grief, after having sparkled but one moment in full light, in order afterwards when it fell into the hands of a sergeant-Tsar, of serf-senators, and chancery-clerks, who have become ministers, to be ruined and crushed!

The design was ingenious, terrible, audacious; for that reason Alexander had chosen it; for that reason it was to be executed. They said the mountain would not support such a church. I do not believe it; particularly if one thinks of the number of new means which engineers in America and England employ in such cases. Tunnels, sometimes of the length of miles; suspension bridges, &c.

Miloradowitch advised Witberg to form the thick columns of the lower temple of granite monoliths. Somebody else objected that the carriage from Finland would be very dear.

"That is just a reason to get them from there", he answered, "if there were granite pits by the river Moscow, there would be nothing extraordinary in erecting them there."

Miloradowitch was a poetical warrior; he understood poetry in general. Grand things are only accomplished by grand means. Nature alone produces great things in vain.

The principal reproach which has been urged against Witberg, even by those who have never doubted his integrity, is the following: "Why did he accept the office of director — he, an inexperienced artist, a youth who did not understand official affairs in the least? He should have been satisfied with the duty of being the architect."

That is true. Such accusations are easily made, if one is tranquilly sitting in one's own room. But he undertook to fulfil that office, just because he was young, inexperienced, an artist; he undertook it, because the Tsar himself offered it to him, encouraged, and supported him. Whose head would not have been turned under such circumstances? Where are those moderate, cool, sober natures? and, if there were such, they would not produce colossal plans — they would never cause "stones to speak."

It is quite natural that Witberg was soon surrounded by a lot of deceivers, by people who look upon Russia, as a matter of business; upon service, as a profitable way of jobbing; upon office, as an opportunity to enrich themselves. It is not difficult to understand that they would try to undermine the ground beneath Witberg's feet; and, in order to render it impossible for him to rise again, if once thrown down, it was necessary that the envy of some, and the wounded self-love of others, should be associated with theft.

The companions of Witberg in the Committee, were the metropolitan Philaret, the Governor-general of Moscow, and the senator Kuschnikoff. They all felt, from the beginning, offended at being associated with a saucy young man, who, moreover, spoke his opinions freely, and opposed the opinions he did not share.

These persons first helped to bring him into a scrape, to calumniate him; and then they threw him, cold-bloodedly, into ruin. The success of these machinations was promoted by the fall of the philonystic ministry of Prince Galitzin, and by the death of the Emperor Alexander.

With the ministry of Galitzin, fell, at the same time, Freemasonry, Bible Societies, and Lutheran pietism; which, all together, had been developed, especially by Magnizki, at Kasan; and Runitsch, at St. Petersburg, till they attained a terrible deformity, brutal and wild persecutions, convulsive ecstasies, insanity, and heaven knows what miraculous things besides.

Rude, rough, and ignorant orthodoxy, took the lead. It was particularly preached by the Noviangorod Archimandrite Fotius, who lived on particularly, although platonically, confidential terms with the Countess Orloff. She, the daughter of the famous Alexis Orloff, who strangled Peter III., thought she could redeem the soul of her father, by giving Fotius and his monastery the greater part of her immense property, which the Empress Catherine had taken by force from the monasteries; and by giving herself up to exaggerated bigotry.

One thing, however, wherein the St. Petersburg government is always constant, whatever change occurs in their principles and faith, is unjust persecution. The madness of Runitsch and Magnizki, recoiled upon the Runitschs and Magnizkis. The Bible Society, but yesterday favoured and prized, as the support of morality and religion, is, today, closed, sealed, and made felony. The "Messenger from Sion", yesterday recommended to all fathers of families, is, today, prohibited worse than Voltaire and Diderot; and its editor, Labsin, banished to Wologda.

The fall of Galitzin is followed by that of Witberg. Everybody now attacks him; the Committee complain; the Metropolitan is offended: the Governor-general very discontented. Witberg's answers are said to be too bold (in his trial, "boldness" is one of the chief accusations); his subordinates are accused of theft — as if, in Russia, it was not known that every official steals. But it is to be presumed, that under Witberg's superintendence, there was more theft than usual; for he was too little accustomed to superintend houses of correction and bands of titled thieves.

Alexander ordered Araktjiyeff to examine into the affair. He pitied Witberg, and sent him word by one of his confidants, "that he was convinced of his innocence."

But Alexander died, and Araktjiyeff fell. Witberg's cause immediately took a bad turn under Nicholas. During ten years, the trial was prolonged, under incredibly absurd pretences. Points of accusation which had been acknowledged by the Court of Justice, were ignored by the Senate. Other points, upon which the Court of Justice justified him, were relied upon by the Senate. The Ministerial Committee entertained every accusation. The Emperor, availing himself of the "best privilege of Monarchs — to pardon, and to soften punishment", added to the sentence — exile to Wiatka.

And so, Witberg went into exile. His sentence is accompanied by the following reasons: —"Dismissed from service for abuse of the confidence with which he was honoured by the Emperor Alexander, and on account of the losses which he occasioned to the Exchequer."

These losses were estimated at about one million roubles. His fortune was sequestrated, his property publicly sold, and rumours were spread, that he had secured immense sums of money in America.

I lived two years in the same house with Witberg, and have since had continual intercourse with him till my departure. He had not even saved enough to ensure his daily bread; his family lived in the utmost poverty.

To characterize this, and all similar affairs in Russia, I will cite a few episodes which are particularly impressed on my memory. Witberg had bought a forest from the merchant Lobanoff, as part of the necessary material for the cathedral. But before the cutting of the wood had begun, Witberg saw another forest, which also belonged to Lobanoff, and was situated nearer the river. He proposed to the proprietor to exchange the one already bought for the other. The merchant agreed to it. The forest was felled, and the wood floated down the river to its place of destination. Afterwards it was found necessary to buy an additional forest, and Witberg re-purchased the first. This affair was made use of, in order to accuse Witberg of having bought the same wood twice. The unfortunate Lobanoff was immured in a house of correction, where he died.

The second episode took place before my own eyes. Witberg bought some landed property for the church. His idea was that the serf peasants, who were bought together with the ground, should be obliged to furnish a certain number of workmen from amongst themselves; and, in return, the village should be made free. It is amusing that our senators, who are all landed proprietors, looked upon this measure as upon a sort of slavery.

Amongst other lands, Witberg intended buying a property belonging to my father, situate in the district of Rus, on the banks of the river Moscow. In this village, marble had been found, and Witberg asked permission to make a geological examination, in order to determine its quantity. My father consented. Thereupon, Witberg set off for Petersburg, and left the examination to the care of a commission.

About three months later, my father learns that the quarrying was already going on in grand style, and that the autumn fields of the peasants were all covered with marble. He protested against it, but was not attended to. A lawsuit, obstinately carried on, ensued. At first the whole blame was put on Witberg's shoulders; but unluckily it was found that he had given no order, and that the committee had done it during his absence.

The affair came before the Senate. To the astonishment of all, the Senate decided pretty reasonably. The broken stones were to be left to the landed proprietor, and the labour of stone-breaking should be accounted to him as a set-off for the devastated fields. The sum of about a hundred thousand roubles, given out by the Exchequer, was to be remitted by the contractors for the works. But the contractors were the companions of Witberg in the building committee — Prince Galizin, Philaretes, and Kushnikoff. There was, of course, much noise and alarm about it. The affair was brought before the Emperor.

This latter has his own jurisprudence.

He ordered all the guilty to be exonerated from payment, "as", thus he wrote it with his own hand, and thus it is printed in the memorial of the senate, "as the members of the committee were not cognizant of what they subscribed their names to." Assuming that the metropolitan, in keeping with his office, ought to display humanity, what is there to be said of the other great lords, who accepted a present so civilly and graciously accounted for.

But now the question is, whence obtain the hundred thousand roubles? The property of the state, it is said, can neither be burnt in the fire, nor drowned in the water. We could add, it can only be stolen. Why reflect long about the matter? Quick! a general adjutant was sent to Moscow to examine the affair.

The adjutant Strekaloff examined, regulated, arranged and terminated the whole in a few days. The stones should be taken from the landed proprietor as set-off for the sum paid for breaking the stones. Should, however, the landed proprietor wish to keep the stones, then he should be obliged to pay a hundred thousand roubles. A particular remuneration was not to be granted to the landowner, as the value of his property had been so considerably augmented by discovering a new source of riches upon it (this is a masterly idea!); but to compensate for the ruin of the peasant's fields, a certain sum of kopecks was to be paid per acre, according to an ukase given by Peter I. about inundated meadows. You see that the party really punished in the affair was my father. It is, however, superfluous to say that, in the process, the stone-quarrying was placed to Witberg's account.

*****

Some years after Witberg's exile, the merchants in Wiatka resolved to build a new church.

To kill every spark of independence, individuality, and imagination everywhere, and in every one, Nicholas has had a whole volume of church facades issued, under the sanction of his supreme will. Whoever wishes to build a church, must necessarily choose one of the governmental plans. People say the Emperor had forbidden Russian operas to be written, having found that those written by the Adjutant Lvoff, in the third division of the imperial chancery, were not worth a farthing. But that is not sufficient. Why should he not also publish a collection of melodies, under sanction of the supreme taste?

The merchants of Wiatka were bold enough, whilst looking at the approved plans, not to coincide with the Emperor's taste. They asked permission to build a church, not only at their own expense, but also according to their own plan. The design presented by them astonished the Emperor; he confirmed it, and ordered the magistrates of the district not to spoil the idea of the architect in any way in the execution.

"Who made this design?" he asked the Secretary of the State.

"Witberg, your Majesty!"

"Who? That Witberg!"

"The same, your Majesty."

And lo! the permission to return to Moscow, or to Petersburg, fell like a tile from the roof upon Witberg's head. The man had asked permission to justify himself; he had been refused. Now, the artist made a successful plan, and the Emperor ordered him to return from exile, as though anybody had ever doubted his talent.

In St. Petersburg, perishing in penury, he made a last effort to defend his honour. It failed entirely. He had applied to Prince Galitzin; but the prince thought it impossible to take up the affair again. He gave Witberg the advice to write a very plaintive letter to the hereditary Grand Duke, and to solicit pecuniary support. He promised to speak for him, together with Jakovsky, and held out to him the prospect of about a thousand roubles. Witberg refused to write the letter.

In the beginning of the winter of 1846, I was, for the last time, in St. Petersburg, and saw Witberg. He was entirely destroyed; even his former scorn for his enemies, which I had liked so much in him, began to disappear. Hopes he had no more; and he undertook nothing to save himself from his unfortunate situation. A dull despair weighed on him; his mind was broken. He waited for death.

If Nicholas intended this triumph, he had every reason to be satisfied.

Is the martyr still alive? I know not, but I doubt it.

"If I had not my family, my children", he said, when I took leave of him, "I would fly from Russia, and wander through the world with the ribbon of my order round my neck, and stretch my hand, with tranquillity, to the passer-by, to ask for charity — that same hand which the Emperor Alexander once pressed — and then I would relate to them my plan, and the fate of an artist in Russia."

"Thy fate, martyr", thought I, "will be known in Europe; I make myself responsible for that."

The connexion with Witberg was a great advantage for me in Wiatka. His serious frankness, and a sort of solemnity in his behaviour towards men, gave him a certain spiritual appearance. He was extremely pure in his morals, and, after all, more inclined to asceticism than to enjoyment. But the rigidity of his character did no injury to the richness and the luxuriance of his artistic nature. He understood how to give his mysticism such a plasticity, such a beautiful hue, that opposition died on your lips; that you would have regretted to analyse, or to criticise the sparkling contour, the misty images of his imagination.

Witberg's mysticism was to be attributed to his Scandinavian blood. It was that same sort of cold reflecting reverie which is to be seen in Swedenborg, and which resembles the fiery reflex of the sunbeams upon the ice mountains of Norway.

Several times, Witberg succeeded in making me hesitate. But my realistic nature soon regained the upper hand. No; it will never be granted to me, to mount up into a third heaven. I am born for quite an earthly existence. No tables turn at the touch of my hand; no rings begin to move at my look. The daylight of thought agrees more with me than the moonshine of imagination. But just at that epoch, when I lived with Witberg, I was more inclined to mysticism than I have been ever since. I was religious, even though my religion had not its origin beyond the stars. How strange and confused is everything in life! In that remote country, in Wiatka, in this filthy official life; in this sad exile, separated from all those whom I loved — what glorious and sacred moments have I spent!